This Living Mirror

This Living Mirror

REFLECTIONS ON CLARE OF ASSISI

❖

SISTER FRANCES TERESA OSC

ORBIS BOOKS

Maryknoll, New York 10545

The Catholic Foreign Mission Society of America (Maryknoll)
recruits and trains people for overseas missionary service.
Through Orbis Books, Maryknoll aims to foster the international
dialogue that is essential to mission. The books published,
however, reflect the opinions of their authors and are not meant
to represent the official position of the society.

© 1995 The Community of Poor Clares, Arundel, West Sussex

First published in Great Britain in 1995 by Darton, Longman and
Todd Ltd, 1 Spencer Court, 140–142 Wandsworth High Street, London
SW18 4JJ

Published in the United States of America by Orbis Books,
Maryknoll, New York 10545–0308

Manufactured in Great Britain

ORBIS/ISBN 1–57075–023–8

Cataloging-in-Publication Data for this book is available from
the Library of Congress, Washington, DC

Contents

❖

The Lord has called us to this greatness: that those who are to be effective mirrors and examples for others, should see themselves mirrored in us ... Therefore, if we have lived according to this form of life which I have already spoken about, we shall leave a noble example to others.

Testament of Clare, 6

Introduction

❖

The central image of this book is St Clare of Assisi's journey to God. Although it began for her, as for us all, even before she was born, for our purposes it started with the born-again experience of her flight from the family home and her consecration to God by St Francis of Assisi. The rest of her life was to be spent on this journey. Because it set a pattern for her whole lifetime, we can see that her flight was a genuinely archetypal journey, effecting an inner transition as well as an outer one. Not only that, but it stands as a model for us as we, too, travel towards God. Many of our journeys, and some of our wanderings, are expressed in hers. Nor is this interpretation far-fetched, for she suggests this inner–outer concordance herself, by often referring to her flight from home as 'the beginning of my conversion'.

It was a journey on many levels. Externally, it was simply a brisk half-hour walk from her family home, but given significance from the fact that she was running away. By this action, she left behind her a whole style of life and embarked on something radically different. Interiorly, it was a transition, a change, from one way of life to another, and therefore it was a rite of passage. It was a death and a birth. It was a journey from the temporal to the eternal, from her natural family to the sisters whom the Lord would give her. It was a journey of identification with Christ, following the command of the letter to the Hebrews that we go to him outside the camp and share his degradation (13:14). It was a classic, mystical journey from isolation into union, the nothingness of poverty becoming a capacity for the Infinite. It was the pursuit of Perfect Joy through an inversion of all previous values.

On our behalf, it was an exercise in spiritual orienteering. People like Clare and Francis are given us to be a compass, pointing always to God. They lay down guidelines for us so that we, too, can find our way from the known to the unknown, from multiplicity to the One, from loneliness to community. They tell us the way. If they do not do this, then however great they may be, they are no use to us. We are called to be ourselves, not to be Francis or Clare, but they have gone before us and left twigs crossed and grasses tied down and stones arranged significantly, so that we can be reassured that we, too, are on the path of Christ as they were. Like all images, this one of Clare's journey is no more than a maypole around which we hang our own bright colours, weaving them into our own patterns as we dance. So I take her flight as a starting point for reflections on the primacy of God in our lives, on rites of passage, on barriers between ourselves and God. A journey is a classic image for a life, just as a wood is a classic image for all sorts of snares and delusions, trials and alarms; and I have used both as a springboard for thinking about the struggles which most of us live with most of the time.

Clare herself said that the Lord had set her as a pattern and an example for others, and this book is an attempt to explore those words and see how they are true for us today, living so long after her. In *Living the Incarnation*, I suggested that prayer falls into three modes, or moods: conversion, contrition and communion, and that each of these is present all the time but with different ones dominating at different stages in our lives. With that ground plan in mind, I have tried to see how those stages of growth and prayer worked out in Clare's own life. For this reason, I have divided the book into three parts under those headings, but they are, to some extent, arbitrary titles, subjective impressions that at *this* time, *that* mode was the primary one.

Reading the generous responses to *Living the Incarnation*, I have been deeply moved by what people have shared with me, but also by the incontrovertible evidence of the pain in which many people live much of their lives. This cannot be glossed over. Instead, we need urgently to learn how pain can become redemptive, so that it can cease to be bitter and destructive and take its rightful place in God's work of creation, redemption and re-creation. Therefore, I have taken Clare's life as the paradigm she said it would be, and within my own prayer allowed it to speak with those who have spoken to me. The more I do this, the more I see that she has indeed been given us by God as a paradigm and a pattern, and also that she seems to be speaking today in a far clearer way than previously. She is emerging into the daylight for us. This is partly the result of scholarly research and interest, but it also seems that she is being discovered by ordinary people (whatever that means) and becoming important to them. She is not a map, I believe, but a compass; she points to the path, to the Way, and says: this is where I walked and this is what happened.

If we see her now as almost the embodiment of peace and joy, we soon realise when we reflect on her story that these did not come easily. Peace and joy are rarely chance emotions but are much more to do with the choices we make. What we all long to know, and hope to learn from her, is how to live in the pain which is a large part of our human condition, but to live in peace and even, on a good day, in joy. Clare experienced the hostility and physical violence of her family, acute pain of bereavement when Francis died, extreme poverty in her daily life, continual ill health and weakness, constant pressure from church authorities to abandon what she felt to be God's call to her. She twice lived through a siege by hostile armies, during one of which her own convent was invaded by Saracen mercenaries. She also saw Francis' ideals become the cause of bitter conflict and anger between his brothers, and herself experienced a certain marginalisation by the authorities because of her uncompromising stand. This seems quite enough to make her some sort of authority on the difficulties of human life! This is the more so when we recall that what her sisters most remembered was that she was never angry or worked up, but always gentle, serene, warm.

She says to us today what Francis said to his brothers as he lay dying: I have done what was mine to do. May God show you what is yours. As we reflect on what was hers to do, it seems reasonable to hope that she will lend a hand in helping us to see what is ours. Not for nothing did her contemporaries equate her with light itself. We live, at the moment, in quite dark days; may she shine for us, as she shone for them, 'giving a clear light in the house of the Lord'.[1]

Below are given some dates pertaining to Clare. A few dates relating to Francis and to some world and church events are included (in italic).

1193/4	Clare Offreduccio di Favarone born
1198	*Uprising in Assisi against the nobility*
1200	*Commune of Assisi established*
	Her family flee to Perugia
1202	*War between Perugia and Assisi*
	Francis captured, imprisoned in Perugia
1204	*Fourth Crusade*
1209	*Innocent III verbally approved Francis' form of life*
1211	Clare and Francis meet secretly
1212	Clare flees from home on Palm Sunday
	She goes to San Paolo, then Sant'Angelo
	She is joined by her sister Catherine
1212	Francis and the brothers take Clare and Catherine (now named Agnes) to San Damiano
1213	*Francis goes to Spain*
1212–15	Francis writes them a Form of Life
1215	Clare 'almost forced' to become Abbess and enclosure introduced at San Damiano
	Magna Carta signed at Runnymede
	Fourth Lateran Council
1216	Clare applies to Innocent III for the Privilege of Poverty
	Bishop Jacques de Vitry in Perugia en route for Holy Land
1217–21	*Fifth Crusade*
1218	Poor Clare communities established at Foligno, Perugia, Florence, Siena, Lucca
1218	Clare and other convents have Hugolino's Rule imposed on them
1219	Agnes goes to Florence as Abbess
	Francis goes to the Holy Land, siege of Damietta
1220	Jacques de Vitry, in a sermon, says the early Poor Clares were not always approved of
	Francis resigns as Minister General
1221	*Francis' First rule (Regula non bullata) written*
1223	*Francis' Second rule (Regula bullata) written*
1224	*Francis receives Stigmata*
	Clare very ill
1225	Francis comes to San Damiano and composes the *Canticle of Creation*

1226   *Death of Francis*
          Carmelite Rule approved

1227   *Probable date of the Sacrum Commercium*
          Twenty central Italian women's communities placed under friars, with the title 'Order of San Damiano'
          Frederick II excommunicated

1228   Cardinal Rainaldo lists twenty-four monasteries of the Order
          Francis canonised
          Sixth Crusade

1229   Florence community granted the Privilege of Poverty

1230   Papal directive: *Quo elongati* forbids the brothers to visit the Poor Clares. Clare reacts strongly
          Crusade of the Teutonic Knights
          Beginnings of the Inquisition

1234   Probable date of Breviary of Clare
          1st and 2nd Letters of Clare to Agnes of Prague
          St Dominic canonised

1238   Prague community granted the Privilege of Poverty and adopts Clare's Rule
          3rd Letter of Clare to Agnes

1240   Saracen invasion

1241   Clare's prayers liberate Assisi from Vitalis d'Aversa

1245   *Council of Lyons*

1246   *Celano's Second Life of Francis published*
          Franciscans first go to China

1247   Rule of Innocent IV imposed on the sisters

1248   *Seventh Crusade*

1250   Innocent IV withdraws his Rule as nobody seems to be keeping it
          Clare's illness enters a more serious phase

1252   Rule written by Clare verbally approved by Cardinal Rainaldo, Protector of the Order

1253   Aug 9, approved by Innocent IV

1253   Aug 11 Clare dies

1255   Clare canonised

1260   The body of Clare transferred to Santa Chiara, within the city walls. The community follow. With time, the memory of her resting place is lost.

1850   Rediscovery of the body of Clare
1872   The body of Clare transferred to Santa Chiara
1893   Rediscovery of the original Papal Bull approving her
       Rule

— PART 1 —
Conversion
❖

Our conversion begins, said St Clare, when we begin to do penance, by which she did not – or not only – mean austerity and self-discipline, but the process of turning our eyes from ourselves unto God. There are blocks between ourselves and God which must be cleared if we are to have an uninterrupted view. There is an inner maze, our personal labyrinth, whose dark ways must be flooded with the light of Christ. There are wild beasts lurking in the woods of life which must be confronted and, if not tamed, at least broken to the plough. All this, the process of conversion, can indeed be penance, and it begins in that moment when we first turn our mind and heart to God – and what is that but the simplest (and arguably the best) definition of prayer?

We can see this process at work in Clare of Assisi, just as we can use her in the way she told us to, as a mirror in which to see ourselves engaged on the same struggle. In this mirror, we can compare our own fuzzy outlines with her clear image reflected there. She is most truly like an elder sister, warning us in advance of the obstacles and hazards we shall meet. If we keep our ears pricked to catch her voice, she will continue to call us forward so that we learn how to go from good to better, from strength to strength.

— 1 —

Life in Abundance

❖

Into my heart's night
Along a narrow way
I groped; and lo! the light,
An infinite land of day.*

The basic story of our universe is a story about God, creator of heaven and earth, who saw all that had been made and found it very good. It is a story of great love, and all the tales of history are only commentaries on it. It is a story about God who is present in our world, rather as heat from the glowing heart of the earth is, they say, present in the depths of the cold Atlantic. Through fissures in the sea bed, it bubbles upwards far more powerfully than the cold weight of water can press downwards. In a similar way, life in abundance bubbles unquenchably into our impoverished hearts, rising up from unimaginable depths. The process by which we learn to live in that abundant life is prayer.

The story of Clare of Assisi is the account of how she learnt to live life in abundance. As her story develops, we see her emerge as a woman of great stature and immense tenderness. She speaks to us about the unquenchable vitality of God, and how it changed her life and those around her. Woven into her story is Francis of Assisi, and the example of their love for God and each other is surely given us by way of encouragement in the risky business of loving God and each other. Clare and Francis do not speak to us about our disintegrating society nor about our mistakes, nor do they speak about how much can go wrong, especially with love. They simply speak about God's great love for us, and their growing wonder and admiration for God. In their relationship with us, they are like mythological heroes who have returned from the Underworld transfigured, offering their transfiguration as a proof of the story they are telling us. They realised that by their Yes to God, they had been caught up in an archetypal narrative in which the hero, Christ, travels

---

* Jalalud-din Rumi, a Sufi mystic and poet, 1207–1273.

even to the halls of hell and yet still returns to the light of Brother Sun.

When we say our Yes to God, we too become caught up in this drama, and Francis and Clare are there to spur us on when it strikes us that we might have acted with foolish rashness. If we let them, they will act as our guides in the journey until the day when we join them in drinking the new wine of the Kingdom. They offer us an assurance that we too can find that wine-cellar of secret communication; that we too can find the divine intoxication of life in abundance. If we are serious in wanting this from them, then we must read their story on two levels, that of the events and that of the message for our own lives. We must compare what they did with what we do. Like genius in any field, these religious geniuses of our history open up new perspectives for the rest of us, just as colour will never be the same since the Impressionists, nor the organ sound the same since Messiaen. What Francis and Clare will teach us is love; not only how to love God but how lovable God is, not only how to catch fire from God but how fiery God can be.

Our understanding of the background to Clare and Francis has been greatly enhanced by modern research into the vigorous women's movements of the early thirteenth century. It seems likely that Clare's (probably widowed) mother, Ortolana, and a group of friends, were living some form of very committed Christian life in their own homes. This may have been on the model of a Beguinage, which was an unstructured grouping of lay people, married or single, who shared a life of Christian commitment and prayer. Such groups sat lightly to the institutional approach and were often frowned upon by the hierarchy who found them too independent. That Ortolana and her friends lived like this is an inference rather than a hard fact, but they were certainly a group of mutually supportive women, struggling beyond the ordinary with faith, prayer and social problems.

One important facet of their spirituality was the pilgrimage. A hundred and fifty years later, Chaucer writes of the Wife of Bath that she:

> ... thrice had been at Jerusalem;
> She has passed many a strange stream;
> At Rome she had been and at Galicia,

> At Saint James and at Cologne,
> Much did she know of wandering by the way.[1]

Apart from the wider implications of wandering by the way,
Ortolana was just like the Wife of Bath; she too had been to
Rome and Saint James in Compostella, as well as Monte Gar-
gano in Italy. She had also been *outre-mer*, across the seas, to
the Holy Land. This was a dangerous but popular voyage, an
indication of the interest in Christ's homeland generated by
the Crusades. There was a certain lady called Bona, living in
Pisa, who used to organise these trips, setting up pilgrimages
with all arrangements taken care of, and such journeys would
do much to bond a group of women together as they shared
hardships and risks and, sometimes, real danger. Pilgrimages
tended to stamp the pilgrims' spirituality with characteristic
devotion, much as Lourdes and Medjugorje do today. Ortolana,
for instance, told some of the sisters that when she had been
pregnant with Clare, she had prayed before the crucifix for a
safe delivery – even less certain then than now. It was only
during the previous century that the crucifix had become so
central in Christian devotion, one indication of the new
religious consciousness sweeping Europe. The crucifix spoke
particularly to women because it symbolised their imaginative
identification with Christ in his pain, and their realisation that
Christ was with them in their pain. This sense of personal
identification was nourished by walking the roads that Christ
had walked and seeing the actual places which fill the pages of
the Gospels.

These were also years when devotion to the veil of Veronica
was spreading. Tradition held that as Christ had passed through
Jerusalem on his way to crucifixion, a woman named Veronica
had stepped out of the crowd and compassionately wiped his
face with a cloth. When she had looked at the cloth later, the
image of Christ's features had been miraculously imprinted on
the material. This cloth, known as the veil of Veronica, had
come to light during these years and had become a focus of
devotion. The story had been brought back to Europe by the
Crusaders, to whom it epitomised all they were fighting for. In
Clare's time, the Cathedral of San Rufino in Assisi had a chapel
dedicated to the Holy Face, with a painting of the veil of Veronica which was taken once a year in procession around Assisi.

We know this because we still have the breviary-missal used by Clare giving the rubrics for this procession. These childhood influences nourish and stamp our imagination for a lifetime, and in fact it is possible to discern their transfigured presence in Clare's later mystical theology. The veil of Veronica, devotion to the Holy Face of Jesus, love for the cross and the custom of pilgrimages brought the Gospel to life for ordinary lay people. Women's education in particular was largely based on lives of the saints and romantic tales of virtuous (or otherwise) ladies. The better educated, like Clare, would have learned to read and write, which means to read and write Latin. The religious currents of the time acted on theology like a Gulf Stream of warm and loving spirituality, marked by a very practical love towards those in need and a great tenderness for the crucified Christ. Many women found a new sense of self-worth through their relationship with Christ, and this affected the way they thought about themselves and their position in society. This was the period and the background against which the concept of an individual self was developing, and although people still defined themselves in terms of their group or society, the long journey of the European consciousness towards individualism had begun, and women were already seeking their place in this development.

So we see that Clare lived at a time not unlike ours in a number of ways. We also see that her religious background was far from mediocre. She was like a musical prodigy who comes, we discover, from a long line of musical people. Given this background, we may well ask why she thought it necessary to escape from her home at dead of night and secretly accept consecration at the hands of Francis; why she thought it necessary to work as a servant in the great Benedictine monastery of San Paolo, why she endured so much from her family and why she lived all her life in genuine indigence and hard work. The simplest answer is that she heard a clear call from God to be a mirror reflecting Christ's complete self-emptying, reflecting the way he had emptied himself of glory and become one of us. Her profoundly apostolic task was to mirror forth this self-emptying. It was a bold and a new leap in imitation of Christ and it was this which required such a complete break. She was being called to more than piety; she was being summoned into the foolishness of God, by which the whole substance of God's house was given for love and counted as nothing. In one of her letters she spells out the purposes of Christ which she had been invited to share:

> It was so that those who were even poorer and needier (starving to death in fact for lack of this heavenly food) it was so that, in him, such people might be enriched by possessing the kingdom of heaven.[2]

Like all the early Franciscans, she was deeply marked by a spirituality of exchange, by which God shared what we are so that we can share what God is; Christ became poor to make us rich; Christ entered our emptiness to open a doorway onto God's fullness. What a great and praiseworthy piece of commerce, she said.[3] By sharing the self-emptying of Christ, Clare herself became an incarnation of humanity's vast capacity for God, and, with maturity, her insights around this central transaction developed into theological thinking of a very high quality. As a theologian, she was quite untrained, but her ideas ring true because they emerged from her lived experience. They are trees rooted in the ground of daily life, rather than balloons of ideas floating off into the stratosphere. She was a highly intelligent woman, subtle, abstract and imaginative, balancing these qualities with a remarkably warm love. She was like a clear window and all who met her were enlightened, as if through her they saw the glory of God for a brief moment. Her contemporaries often spoke of her in terms of light or brightness and clarity, playing joyfully and affectionately with her name, Clara or Chiara in Italian.

For her, as for us, God's plan was only slowly revealed, and only fully revealed in the Kingdom that is not yet. We only learn with difficulty that no matter how soaring our ideals, it is in ordinary life that they must first be realised. The vision of the Kingdom is at ground level: Christ washes our feet. For Clare and Francis, that passage in John's Gospel where Jesus washed the disciples' feet came to have deep significance. They saw this act as the single distinguishing attitude of Christian service, and above all of Christian leadership. For them, it summed up the whole of Christ's attitude towards us, his respect, his generous service, his gentle restoration of our tarnished dignity, the way he honours us as people loved by God. This was what Francis advised his brothers to do for those in their care,[4] and what

Clare did quite literally and habitually for her sisters [1:12; 2:3; 10:6].*

Clare was aware that there is all the difference in the world between doing good to people, as she had from her ancestral home, and actually joining them, as Christ had done. It was no part of Clare's concern to make a social statement about wealth or poverty, although her way of imitating the incarnate Word would clearly recommend 'downward mobility'.[5] The barriers between classes, as she knew only too well, work both ways, but the upward barriers were irrelevant because the Gospel told her that the Kingdom of heaven has been given to the poor (Matthew 5:3).

> I believe you know that the Lord has promised and given the Kingdom of heaven to none but the poor, for while we are giving our affections to the transient we are losing the fruit of love,[6]

she wrote to Agnes, Princess of Bohemia. What a reminder about reality for us in our increasingly polarised society! What a transformation would come about if we shared Clare's realisation that she, not the poor, was shut out of the Kingdom. It was she, in the palazzo, who was challenged by Christ's words: I have given you an example so that you may copy what I have done to you – washed your feet (John 13:15). Francis said once that he felt indicted when he saw someone poorer than himself because he knew that the Lord had called him to be the servant of everyone. Clare shared this insight and this call, but while she remained in her aristocratic home, she had no choice but be among those who were served and had their feet washed by others.

Finally, the moment came when she could follow the Word made flesh (John 1:14), the one who had emptied himself to take the form of a servant (Philippians 2:7). She left her home on Palm Sunday, at the start of Passover week, when both Christians and Jews recall the Exodus from Egypt and the long trek to the Promised Land. It was the time when the Church recalls how Christ made that exodus his own, setting his footprints on that paradigm road of all humanity. Clare must have noticed this parallel, for she too was leaving a secure and comfortable

---

* Because there are so many, references to the Canonisation Process have been put in square brackets in the text, thus avoiding a multiplicity of endnotes.

way of life (Egypt, onions and cucumbers) to set out for the
Promised Land in the company of the One who was to be
crucified. There were no maps, only his footprints. She was as
dependent on the daily guidance of God as ever the Israelites
had been and, like the Israelites, she trusted God to bring her
to the Promised Land because she too had gone into the desert
solely in order to worship (Exodus 3:12). For her, as for Israel,
the Promised Lane was both itself and more than itself. It was,
then and always, Adam and Christ, Paradise and Calvary. It is
now and it is not yet. Legend says that Christ's cross was planted
where the tree of knowledge had once grown, and as so often,
legend accurately expresses the mystical spirit of Christianity.
Clare's exodus was short in mileage, half an hour through the
olive groves and woods, but it was a true symbolic exodus. It
fulfilled what the rabbis insist is essential, that this exodus
happen personally for each of us. Ill-prepared though we often
are, we must all leave our country and enter the waste land,
otherwise, the rabbis teach, we shall never come to the Land of
Promise. As Clare understood it, our personal commitment to
that desert journey is expressed through poverty, the means by
which we interiorise the waste land and make it our own. Without this inner exploration of the desert, we shall never see the
pillar of cloud, never taste the manna or wonder at the Sheki-
nah, the glory of God shining on the face of God's Friend.

History tells us that on the night of Palm Sunday, 18 March
1212,[7] Clare slipped unnoticed from her home through one of
those small, side doors at the end of a long, narrow passage
which can still be seen in old Umbrian houses. Some historians
say these doors were only used for the dead, but others think
they were designed as an exit which could easily be defended
by one man. At the time of Clare's flight, the door was
blocked by heavy wooden beams and iron bars, which she
cleared by herself; her unnamed companion seems to have
come along afterwards, presumably from another house. How
was it that Clare was not heard by the night watchman, and was
he the same Ioanni de Ventura, house watchman, who later gave
evidence at her canonisation process? Had he been suborned
by this determined young lady? A friend, who became Sister
Christiana, says that she had been in the Offreduccio home
that night. She was there in the morning when the family came
down and saw the mess and were unable to believe that one

young girl had moved such heavy barriers by herself [13:1]. The full story only broke upon the family by degrees. At first, the powerful and dominant uncles were concerned that Clare had thwarted their plans for her. Later they clamoured that she had disgraced them in the eyes of their circle. They had yet to learn that she had sold all her inheritance and part of her sister's, and given the proceeds to the poor. They had yet to discover that two more sisters and the mother would follow her, not to mention two nieces, some cousins and various childhood friends. They had yet to learn that Clare would be canonised and they would be cast as first villains! Clare realised only too well that most of her family would see her action as a betrayal and a scandal. We are told that although she and Catherine, the sister closest to her, had a great mutual love, there was a 'sorrowful division' between them,[8] and one of the few requests we know she made for herself was that Catherine might join her.

When the blocks were cleared and she stepped into the dark piazza, she came to the moment which she later called 'the beginning of my conversion'. Conversion is not often unmixed joy and she, too, must have felt mingled pain and exaltation. Conversion must include a death of one kind or another or what has changed? Like every exodus, Clare's began with hard lessons in desert living, it was the end of security and comfort, approval and respect. She must have grown up at that moment, knowing that her protected childhood was over. For all she knew, was a definitive and final breach with her mother and sisters as well as with the uncles, and she threw herself on God's care in what Blake calls 'minute particulars' as completely as any sparrow in the hedge. On the other hand, she was eighteen and ready for adventure, and was to prove far too powerful a character ever to have settled meekly into being the chatelaine of even a dozen castles. Educated for a society in which young girls (especially beautiful ones) were counters, if not pawns, in dynastic power games, she was undoubtedly seen as an asset by the family, a long-term investment destined to augment their prestige and fortune. By escaping, she was denying them a future of enhanced authority, something far more important than the price of her inheritance. She must have been aware of this. She must also have been aware that there was a contractual nature to it: if she did her part, her reward would be security,

privilege and comfort, respect, honour and perhaps fame. By
her escape, she forfeited the rewards of conformity and perhaps
our imaginations are right to be caught by the notion that the
small door was only for the dead, because we sense that it really
was a door of death for her on many levels.

She may also have felt twinges of apprehension about the
immediate future, because as the story unravels it becomes
apparent that no plans had been made by these two improvident
saints-to-be. Suddenly, she was homeless, every bit as vulnerable
and at risk as any other young girl out at night with nowhere
to sleep. However confident that God, Francis and the brothers
would not abandon her, she had probably never been out at
night by herself before. It is more than likely that she had never
been alone with men before, as she soon would be, or if she
had, it had certainly not been in the woods at midnight, nor
with men who had abandoned the refinements of life, roughing
it in the name of penance and holy Poverty. All she could do
was to put her trust in God, and in the brothers' commitment
to God. If the brothers were not genuine, she was indeed in
trouble.

She may not have realised at this point that this death and
this risk were only the first of many. While we notionally agree
that our call to prayer is a sharing in the death of Christ, we
never fully absorb the fact that this means our death. Yet it is
the process of dying which makes us apt for glory, just as it
is this journey through the waste land which enables us to enter
the Promised Land, to become the sort of people through
whose lives the radiance of the Incarnation can spread. Years
later, searching for an image to express what she felt God had
done in her life, Clare said that the Lord had made her a mirror
to reflect God's glory to us. She shares little about the process
of being polished for that task, but says that she sees herself as
a mirror set for our encouragement, 'a noble example', she
dared to say, of the light we shall reflect when we too have been
polished – or ground, as we may feel. The essence of her life,
she is saying, is to encourage us when the going becomes rough.

There is another aspect to this journey of Clare's which also
touches our own journey. This is that her flight has all the
hallmarks of a rite of passage. It is not only a journey from one
place to another, but also a journey from one state or condition
to another. It is a transition from adolescence to maturity, from

being a marriageable young girl to a fruitful woman, from conformity to the values of others to self-reliance on her own heart
and conscience. By this transition, she becomes a spiritual
leader, and her stature as a leader will prove to be every bit as
great as the transition has been. Now, her potential can develop,
and the enlightenment which follows any rite of passage begins
to dawn on her. Every rite of passage both links and divides the
past and the future; it is like an airlock, and the symbolic journey
through this airlock ushers us into an enlargement of spirit. It
is one of the hallmarks of it that there is no way back, growth
cannot be un-grown, the old ways have become impossible. The
airlock is a one-way passage. So it is a true death and a genuine
rebirth through which we enter a new relationship with our
own story. Because it has changed us, we now understand things
differently. What was impossible before, may now be easy. The
period of transition can feel like total confusion and its full
dimensions may only be revealed to us slowly, but whenever we
find ourselves understanding our story and ourselves in a new
way, then that is a hint that we may be emerging from a rite of
passage. After months as a chrysalis, a long gestation will bring
us, as it brought Clare, to the threshold of new life.

That journey through the houses of Assisi, her unexplained
exit through the (presumably shut) gates of the city, her flight
through the farms and olive groves and so to the uncultivated
woods around St Mary of the Angels, were like a sacrament:
they brought about what they symbolised. Leaving her security
and travelling through dark places into the light, she moved
from solitude to community, from bondage to freedom. Like
the Israelites, she had waited for midnight, dressed for the
journey, trusting that God would lead her to the Promised
Land. The call to Abraham, the Exodus from Egypt and Jesus'
invitation to follow him, had merged into one imperious and
irresistible summons, and in response she had thrown herself
into the hands of God. She was a leaf entrusted to the wind of
the Spirit. It was the beginning of her conversion. She had
heard and believed the Word and she was setting out to live life
in abundance.

What a great and praiseworthy piece of commerce.[9]

2

Exodus

❖

From now on I will only say: our Father in heaven.*

This great and praiseworthy piece of commerce became a central theme for Clare, but what was it, what was the commerce, this exchange? In its widest expression, it is to exchange slavery to sin for the service of Jesus Christ. Clare's imagination was always very concrete, and she pictured this service of Jesus Christ as a place, a definite condition which we enter and which changes us as we live in it. Probably her imagination was influenced by the feudal situation where the young knight-to-be would enter the service of a great lord, as a result of which his life underwent radical changes. From then on, he would live in the lord's house and serve him in quite menial ways besides learning the skills of battle, fired all the time by the hope of winning his spurs. Such servitude was tolerated by these proud young men because they recognised it as the path to glory.

Clare explored the spiritual implications of all this, enriching her thought with St Paul's insights about the Christ who exchanged his glory for the condition of a slave. This was the service of Jesus Christ which Clare now entered and she became the household servant, the *famula*, of Christ and all who serve him. The difference is that she was even more of a servant than that, choosing to do what Christ had done as literally and profoundly as possible. The initiative for this comes from God, for us as for her. God is the one who first called her into the service of the poor, crucified one. 'Poor', in Clare's language, is not a word of easy sympathy but a statement of reality. Christ is poor because he is totally generous, for poor and generous are almost synonyms to her. God is the truly poor one because God is the totally generous one. She advises us to give this our mature reflection; we are called to imitate God in this

---

* St Francis of Assisi.

or, at least, to do so as far as in us lies. The crucified Christ is
the source of energy for such a servitude, for in Christ all the
vast designs of God reach their culmination, Christ is the one
in whom all our lives are caught up. His is the praiseworthy
piece of business.

If we take Clare's advice and think this over, we realise that
this mystery happens in our own lives, too. When she speaks of
'mature' reflection surely she means that we reflect on what
God is doing, rather than on what God is doing for me. By
doing this, we learn to recognise God's style and we acquire a
feel for God. This helps to free our hearts so that we can forget
ourselves and see how God has entered our littleness in order
to offer us greatness of a new kind. We begin to see the power
and passion of that offer, we begin to see the burning desires
of Christ. We often think that our lowliness, poverty and weakness (to use three words much used by Clare) are our problem
and even our sin, aspects of ourselves we would rather be without, but the Incarnation of Christ offers a disturbing hint that
this may be an illusion, and even a mistake. God has entered the
heart of our muddle and given it life in abundance, recreating it
from within, a method which Clare and Francis, who were
familiar with God's style, called God's holy manner of working.
Clare saw that when we work together with Christ, then even
our weakness and wounds become means of redemption for
others. With Christ, we endure these wounds and weaknesses,
which were once cracks in our defences, and we discover that
through the power of the poor and crucified one, our weaknesses and wounds can become the sort of cracks through which
grace floods for others. This is the alchemy of him who explored
the margins of human weakness as no one else has ever done.

Again and again, Clare's writings reveal her awareness of the
difference between God's thoughts and ours. The range of her
vision, even in these early years, is astounding, for her perception of God was an insight into great beauty, immense vitality
and surpassing tenderness. One of the words she loves to use
about prayer is *considerare*, originally connected with star-gazing,
or so it is thought. Star-gazing at God, we look into the heart
of things and are changed by that gazing. God is such a fragrance as to bring even the dead to life again, she says, and this
might well include us. Dead though we can feel in spirit or in
heart, the fragrance of God irresistibly stirs life within us, like

the smell of the distant sea to one too far inland, encouraging
us to take further steps on our long exodus from bondage to
freedom, from pain to joy, from death to life in abundance.

It is he whose love stirs us to love,
whose contemplation remakes us,
whose kindliness floods us,
whose sweetness fills us,
whose memory glows gently,
whose fragrance brings the dead to life again.
The glorious vision of him has made most blessed
all the citizens of the Jerusalem from above,
since she, Jerusalem, is the splendour of eternal glory,
the brightness of everlasting light
and an unspotted mirror.
Gaze into this mirror daily, and continually reflect your own face in it.[1]

These words, written so long ago, are still valid, as love poems
from another era remain valid long after the lovers have fallen
silent. Let us learn from them if we dare. Clare did what we
long to do – she spoke with the living God in the doorway of
her tented humanity. This same living God seeks us too, gently
enticing us from the dark recesses of our tent. In almost every
life, there seem to be those dark areas of bondage which we
inhabit with distaste and leave with reluctance. When we hear
the voice of the living God speaking in that lost part of ourselves,
we often behave like Adam and Eve, looking for somewhere to
hide. We are not eager to enter a desert wilderness which feels
to us like loss and deprivation. Like the Israelites, we have this
terrible tendency to prefer onions and cucumbers to the living
God. Yet leave we must; God is the one thing necessary and
Clare, reminding us of this, says that she bears witness to this
one thing necessary.[2] This is what she thought her life was about,
and also the meaning of her life for us – that she witnesses to
the one thing necessary. If we heed her words, then when we
finally come to the mountain of the true Jerusalem, we will not
need to look for a ram caught in the bushes, because we ourselves will be the gift that God is seeking. The terrible days
when we braced ourselves to slaughter Isaac, the child of our
laughter, eventually pass. Our conversion may take a lifetime,
but at least it has begun and we will quickly discover that freedom is accretive. Each step forward makes possible other steps
which were previously impossible, and all this has been brought

about by the 'burning desire of the Crucified' for the gift of our heart's love.

That midnight moment when Clare emerged from the narrow passage-way of her home and stood in the piazza, free and reborn, is an analogue of the moment when Francis stripped off all his clothes and gave them back to his father, saying, 'From now on I will only say: our Father in heaven.' Standing in the doorway, Clare could say the same: 'From now on I will only say: our Father in heaven.' Now she could live in total trust, and from this time on, her communication with God would be the primary dialogue of her life. We tend to link the powerfully romantic aura about her life to her relationship with Francis, but this is a mistake, although the romance is genuine. It was God, the Source, who was the overwhelming passion of Clare's life. Francis was what her biographer calls him, a marriage broker! He was the friend of the bridegroom. Clare's enlightenment was a revelation to her heart about God, about the quality of God's love for her, and about the nature of the response she wished to make. In the steadfastness of this love, she is our leader and teacher, as well as our mirror.

Unlike most of us who go forwards and backwards, 'tacking against contrary winds' we say hopefully, it seems that Clare never lost ground once gained, so complete was her response. The fruit of her enlightenment was that she entrusted herself totally to the one who loved her totally. She said that Jesus, by sharing his Spirit with us, has so bound us to himself that, man or woman, we cleave to him as closely as two people cleave to each other in marriage. The word she uses for cleave is *adhaerere*, the word used in Genesis 2:24 about a man cleaving to his wife; just so do we cleave to Christ and he to us. We cling to Christ by following in his footsteps: cleaving to his footprints, Clare says,[3] and it is this which gives us life. When we cease denying that we are impoverished, we can begin sharing in the poverty of Christ by which we, who were starving to death, can be filled with good things. When we thought we were rich, we could only come away empty. Poor, we can share in the Godhead. The significance of being poor shifts from not having, to having given. Love him totally; cease to be acquisitive. Both poverty in God and generosity in us are one act of sharing, just as our poverty and the vast generosity of God are one cyclic reality.

Such sharing is one of the skills of Jerusalem, however, and first there are the Red Sea and the Sinai desert to cross. Nor will we cross them once only, but over and over again, because that journey of Israel is the pattern of all our journeys into God, who is infinite. The desert not only reveals the infinities of the Godhead, but also the vast distances between us and God. In the wilderness, we are cut down to size and sculpting forces engrave the features of Christ on us, like the brand of our redemption. Truth cuts deeper and deeper into the shifting dunes of our being. As human beings, it is our privilege and our problem that we are summoned into a greatness beyond us. We are always being forged again in the furnace, hammered out on the anvil of events and plunged again and again into experiences of death, in order to make us apt for abundant life.

The stones which blocked Clare's doorway, the door of death, represent the many forms of our experiences of death. Often, the power of such blocks is only revealed when we try to move – or remove – them. Worse than that, our parasitic hearts become entwined around them; we so easily grow addicted to the familiar, however awful, and only experience the pain when we try to break the addiction. The truth is, though, that while we are steeped in disorder we are numb and do not feel the pain. Only when we start tackling things do we feel the full force of both the disorder and the pain. While the disorder is in control, we have no sense of it and are deterred from tangling with it by this ultimate deterrent of pain. Becoming free can feel as if the bones of our minds are being broken and reset and, in fact, this is an apt simile. Yet without this process, how shall we cripples leap before the Lord? We have to suffer these things and so come into our glory (Luke 24:26). Only when I am stripped naked can redemption clothe the flesh of my life, only when I acknowledge my poverty can I begin to realise that the truth will set me free.

From this scrutiny of our own hearts, we learn about the struggles of other hearts. In that scrutiny of hearts, unsuspected aspects of ourselves may delight us, or we may find truths buried which completely change the way we think about ourselves and we may have to live for a time in incommunicable pain, no longer sure who we are. At such a time, all our relationships will be reshuffled and every goal post moved. At such a time, we can reassure ourselves that, in spite of all appearances to the contrary, we will not always feel as we do now. Now we feel

outraged that others smile and laugh while we struggle with
terrible memories and terrified feelings, and our prayer at such
a time may well be raw emotion. This is good, a major shift into
greater honesty. God, more than anyone else, understands our
shouts of anger and pain; shares them, perhaps. God is a father
in defensive outrage for us, a mother in tenderness while we
fall apart and flounder. Once we have emerged from this caul-
dron, that gift of honesty will remain with us, though all else
may change. That is why spiritual guides insist that this is no
time for decisions. Let decisions stand until the dust settles,
when everything can be reconsidered, but for the moment the
tranquillity of order is on the other side of the moon. It will
not always be like this because happiness will return to us. We
will be led out again from our tortured battleground, but this
time we will come from our desert places bearing gifts, like the
Magi. We shall look back and see how the prophecy of Isaiah
has been fulfilled in us:

> They are to be called 'terebinths of integrity',
> planted by the Lord to glorify him.
> They will rebuild the ancient ruins,
> they will raise what has long lain waste,
> they will restore the ruined cities
> all that has lain waste for ages past. (Isaiah 61:3,4)

The awareness of change is always profoundly disconcerting,
and we miss our secure addictions. Even Clare, we find, went
for a while from place to place, aimless, waiting, with no peace
of mind, seeking for she knew not what. The whole skill of
blocks lies in persuading us that they are essential, or even
normal. The Offreduccio family found an impassable back door
quite normal; what seemed abnormal was that Clare cleared it
and went out. Had they been asked, they would probably have
said what we all say, that it could easily be cleared at any time,
but in fact the dynamite of the Spirit was needed. We, now, can
see that the significance of the Offreduccio doorway is precisely
that it was cleared. Had it not been, who would have remembered it eight hundred years later? Who could have guessed
that it was as important to Clare as the Red Sea crossing for
Israel, or the confrontation with his father to Francis? Who
could have realised that it was the beginning of Passover for
her?

All through that strange Passover month, Clare took great leaps in experience, one after the other. To become a co-worker of Christ, she set out in the darkest hour of the night, at the darkest season of the Christian year, at the low ebb of all the natural cycles. This archetypal journey through the passion and death of Christ to the resurrection became the ground-plan of her life. For the rest of her days she would retrace it, like an artist perfecting a line, over and over, until her identification with Christ was complete. She became so rooted in Christ and so identified with him, that she could finally say to her sisters: I am a hostage for you – and hostile soldiers on seeing her would fall back, overcome by alarm, as other soldiers had seen another hostage in another garden and fallen back before him onto the ground (John 18:6).

She herself calls this exodus 'the beginning of my conversion'. She had left a way of life to which she could no longer subscribe, to seek one which expressed the value system she believed to be God's. Liberation theologians have made us much more aware of the sinful drives, greeds and obsessions on which any society is built, and Clare herself had found that the values of her social group were no longer tenable, at least by her. She needed to abstract herself from a life based on acquisition and exploitation and to imitate the generosity of God. She made no judgements of others; it was simply that compromise had become intolerable to her for she had embarked on a search for *honestas* – for integrity, grace, character, a quality which she valued highly and recommended often and which has no exact English equivalent. Originally, an *honestamentum* was an ornament, then the word began to be used for a grace of style, a literary ornament, and hence to imply a moral ornament, a reputation, character and probity. It means the whole grace of integrity and all the integrity of grace.

Like Israel, she heard God's command to Pharaoh: let my people go to offer me worship (Exodus 4:23). This is said to every Pharaoh in every society, as well as to the Pharaoh in our own household and, above all, to the Pharaoh in our own hearts. It is a word of revelation because it reveals that we are not yet free to worship even though we are created for worship. So it challenges us about the easy way we settle down in the securities of slavery (onions and cucumbers), the contented way we live with radically diminished lives. Both in societies and individuals, worship nourishes our true freedom, and that freedom withers when it is cut off from its taproot. God is our only trustworthy guarantor of freedom, be it personal or political. Clare, even though she was living the devout life in her home, was not fully able to worship the poor Christ as she felt called. For that to happen, she had to break chains and bonds, within and without. She had to remove barriers from the doorway and barriers from her heart. She had to escape, to be pursued and hounded, harassed and rescued, she had to wander in an inner wilderness until she came to San Damiano.

 The first and most vital lesson that these experiences of Clare teach us is that prayer and life are a seamless garment. Just as we learn to love by loving, so we learn to worship by worshipping, by star-gazing on God. In the process, our focus shifts, our lives change and we enter the Promised Land. Work begins then on the restoration of Paradise, but she warns us not to make heavier weather of our exodus than we need:

> Step lightly without stumbling, and believe nothing, agree with nothing which would make you want to recall your purpose or which would place a stumbling block on your path.[4]

This alertness, this stepping lightly but without stumbling, enables us to run towards God faster and faster, raising no dust as we go. This alertness is a desert skill, learnt in the wilderness where we feel under threat and at bay, but are really being forged into the people of God. Clare's life shows us that God fits events both to our weakness and to our greatness. She was simultaneously nurtured tenderly and challenged to go further, tried to the top of her bent, but at every turn her true needs were always met. In time she came to that watershed after which psychological and spiritual growth begin to help each other. Although, in fact, they were always on a converging course, they can seem so far apart that we experience them as stealing energy from each other instead of helping each other.

Conversion begins with God. The Father of mercies graciously enlightens our hearts, and this is not just for ourselves but, says Clare, as a mirror for all those living in the world[5] and also, as she reminds Agnes, for the people of the future – us.[6] In this glass, we see her being led into the secret wine-cellar and there, like wisdom, she reflects the workings of God. God is a lover, who invites us to taste the rarest vintage, stored in this secret

cellar to which we cannot come on our own; we can only be
led there by the Master Vintner. Clare and Francis had a dream
that everyone in the world would come to know the beauty and
goodness of God. Though we are sinners, God is full of mercy
and forgiveness and asks only that we want to grow in goodness.
This simple insight was the spring for all their apostolic thrust.
Clare, living her enclosed life, had to find a deeper meaning
for words like mendicant and apostolic, which led her to understand space and time in an interestingly cosmic way, as planes
of being, focused around the figure on the cross. Once she had
thrown in her lot with Christ, the figure on the cross, she
found that she had been catapulted into the heart of humanity's
struggle for freedom. As a result, everything that happened to
her has become an event for us all.

Bernard Lonergan, the Jesuit thinker and writer, has said that
when God speaks to us, the Word always has three aspects or
dimensions.[7] It is a personal Word, spoken to me alone; it is
social, spoken for my time, and it is historical, spoken for all
time. The Word spoken to Clare as personal, for herself alone,
was a word about the mercy and graciousness of God in her
 regard. This was her primary revelation, the moment when God
spoke to her condition and she came to the beginning of her
conversion. It was the beginning of contrition too, that apparently never-ending process of perceiving and grieving over the
gulf between God and what we see in the mirror. It is also where
communion begins, when God reaches out to us across all these
gulfs and invites us into his wine-cellar. When we have felt and
responded to God's mercy, then we can speak to others; the
Word begins to be revealed in its social dimension. This is what
Clare did, sharing with others the kindness and compassion
which she had learnt from the Father of mercies. The Word,
however, is also historical. The truth spoken to Clare and shared
with her sisters, is for us as well. It is a word of encouragement:
the Father is still merciful. It is a word of challenge: God's mercy
implies our sin. Among the many bonds which can bind us to
people like Clare, she would say that the strongest is that we
both share in the mercy of God. This is the foundation of true
community, and on it Clare based her community, as a nucleus
of a much wider grouping extending through time and space.
'If a mother love and nourish her daughter in the flesh,' she

said, 'how much more attentively should a sister love and nourish her sister in the Spirit.'[8]

Here is Clare sharing with us what she had learnt, here is the
Word in its historical dimension – historical in that it has come
down to us through history, and also historical in that the
primary story of the universe is being retold in our personal
lives. It was to give us this Word that Clare was called forth into
the desert. It was to give us this Word that she was led
into confrontation with every imperfection in her own heart so
that she could faithfully repeat God's Word of mercy and grace
to us, the people of her future.

— 3 —

The Minotaur Within

❖

Who would not shrink from the ambush of humanity's enemy,
who schemes to reduce to nothing
that which is greater than the heavens?*

Leaving her home and moving silently through the streets of
Assisi, Clare came down the hill, past the olive groves and
vineyards, to the thick, deciduous wood which surrounded the
tiny chapel of St Mary of the Angels, the Porziuncola or Little
Portion. This chapel, which the Benedictines rented to Francis
for an annual basket of fish, was one of those which he had
repaired. While he was doing so, the young Lady Clare had sent
him some money as an alms, and this is the first indication we
have that they knew about each other [17:7]. Because it became
the birthplace of Francis's Order, it seemed fitting that Clare
should also begin her gospel form of life in the same place. As
a result, it always held a special position in both their hearts;
this little church was truly their mother, for life had begun for
them in that place.

As Clare approached the wood around the chapel, the character of her journey changed. It lost its aspect of flight and became
a journey towards the life about to start. The narrow, blocked
passage-way had indeed been like a birth canal, but now the
trauma of birth was over and life itself was beginning. It was
Monday in Holy Week, early in the small hours. She was emerging from straitened places and coming into the light, reborn in
the Gospel. Her dreams and hopes were waxing to fulfilment,
like Sister Moon, now less than a week from her Easter fullness.
Clare stood on the threshold of a new place, a new time, new
values, a new family and a new life. We have all known such
moments when we are lifted up out of the ordinary and feel
ourselves temporarily transformed by living through a fundamental human experience. We become, for a moment, arche-

---

* Clare, *Letter 3*, 20.

typal figures signifying life, as if we were entering the myth by
which we all live, touching with authority the raw nerve of life.

Every society nourishes itself through rituals and ceremonials
which are all the more powerful when they are not articulated.
These rituals recreate our past and speak to us about our future.
In our western society, such rituals are changing and sometimes
being lost altogether, yet we are still able to understand events
symbolically, can still see a bride, for instance, as more than
simply herself. She still personifies a new springtime for our
exhausted culture. We are content, for a moment, to warm
our hearts at this symbol, content to toast the bride as a promise
for the future because we know that ordinary life will reassert
itself soon enough. For a short time, the bride personifies a
perennially fruitful love which is, we fantasise, always new. This
is why she is such a powerful symbol of renewal. This is why
lovers who transcend social hostilities awaken such deep sympathy in us, because they hold out a promise of unification
where we had thought there was no such possibility.

The image of the bride was to be important to Clare precisely
because she understood this longing for a fresh beginning. She
realised, however, that our expectations will never be fulfilled
in the union between man and woman, but only in that between
God and humanity. Christ and the new Jerusalem is the true
marriage which is the paradigm for the others, and we are all
summoned into this paradigm, she, Francis, the sisters, the
brethren and we ourselves, people of their future, married or
unmarried. She came gradually to a full understanding of all
this, and we can trace her developing theology through her
letters, spanning nearly twenty years. In her last extant letter,
written not long before she died, she draws her thoughts
together, shifting between various levels of union: our individual
union with Christ, God's union with humanity in Christ, and
the gift of human love which reveals these other unions.

From the point of view of her family, these issues were
unspoken but certainly part of their frustrated plans. Clare was
not only robbing them of rites and rituals but of the accompanying renewal of power and energy, and all this stirred energeti-
cally behind their reaction to an act which they saw as beyond
forgiveness. At that time, marriage alliances were an integral
part of the social fabric, and the family felt quite justified in their
anger. It was not simply that they now lacked the considerable

bargaining power of Clare's beauty, status and general desir-
ability, but their violent reaction was further fuelled by the fact
that their supremacy was already under threat in other ways,
disputed not so much by Clare as by society itself. Cracks had
appeared in the fabric of their certitudes. Their conviction of
stability had been threatened, as had their confidence that
the victory of the *maiores* over the *minores*, the nobility over the
citizens, meant a secure and unchanging future for them all.
Above all, she threatened them with change and, like many
institutions under threat, they had not reacted with understanding adjustment and generous accommodation, but with
entrenchment and intransigence. As they saw it, the walls they
had built around themselves were being breached, not from
without but from within, which was doubly alarming. Ideas alien
to their circle had borne fruit within that circle, like some exotic
seed blown over the wall of the keep. A world in which marriage
alliances, female quiescence, power and property were inextri-
cably linked, saw the writing on the wall and fought angrily to
wipe it off.

Clare's family stood at the headwaters of a redefinition of
society, waters in which we today are almost drowning. With us,
even the fundamental morality of the marriage-bond itself is
coming into question, not from some new inability but from a
profound doubt about the right of anyone to ask or give such
a gift. Women, in particular, are rethinking everything, and
thereby obliging men as well to see life from new angles. Perhaps part of Clare's message – for she did something similar –
is a measure of guidance on how to avoid blind alleys and
decisions which are self-destructive. She reminds us that God,
who is here and now, is also the architect of the future. As a
woman who helped to build that future, Clare offers us what
she offered women of her own day: skill in developing new
insights into feminine autonomy and independence, into
renewal and fresh beginnings. She avoided coming to this by
simply reacting against the status quo but, instead, nourished
the vitality of her growth with her experience of God. This is
where her balanced sense of independence and autonomy came
from, this is where she experienced being most creatively loved,
and these gave her so wholesome an individuality that she was
able to find a new way forward into a new future.

It is hard, today, to realise the originality of what she established. The centuries have eroded and smoothed its edges, and for many people Poor Clare life is either unknown or else has been vaguely grouped together with other forms of contemplative religious living. Yet her contemporaries realised it very clearly. The fact of anything being established by a woman was new in itself, and it is quite likely that Francis was aware of this. Like most male religious of the time, he was reluctant to be drawn into too much pastoral work with nuns, but he may also have realised that God was doing a new work in Clare, one for which she was fully competent. Beyond all this, though, was the immense personal stature of Clare herself in the eyes of her contemporaries, a stature which simply grew as the years went on. She was a new leader of women[1] precisely because, having gone through her own ritual of liberation, she was able and qualified to lead others. It is basic to leadership that we can only take others over ground we have ourselves covered.

In order to do this, each of us has a need, almost an imperative, to confront the unknown which lies coiled in the centre of our heart's labyrinth, and it is the role of the spiritual guide to help us to do this. We have an urge to drink from a hidden spring in that secret place within ourselves where both our treasure and our rubbish are stored. Our instinct tells us that, psychologically and spiritually, this is the route to liberation. Following Clare, who followed Christ, we can approach the centre of our maze, where our monster, like a personal Minotaur, hides from the light of day. This is the raw, inglorious material of our still un-glorified humanity. This is where those desires lurk that can startle us into doing things about which we say: I can't think why I did that. While we need torchbearers like Clare, people who know the way, we must also accept that only we ourselves can walk through our own wasteland, or penetrate our own protective maze. This is a personal responsibility which nobody can carry for us, even if our journey through these tracts in our hearts turn out to be our personal harrowing of hell.

The Minotaur is an image for that part of ourselves with which we are secretly fascinated, secretly ashamed and secretly afraid. Much of our fear and fascination stem from our sense that there is an undefined potential here, that this apparent monster holds all that is still to be realised in us, together with much which we sincerely hope will never be realised. We experience this hidden self as a capacity, but also as a force about to escape from control. We feel, quite rightly, too uncertain about whether it is good or evil to let it roam freely in the streets of our minds, although, in fact, the forces we sense in ourselves are neither good nor evil but potent with either. There are choices to be made, and they are entirely ours. Until we have made these choices, the image of the maze will remain both an obstacle and a protection. The puzzle of the maze has to be unravelled without tearing down necessary defences. It is like a personalised nuclear base which we must dismantle without releasing nuclear energy into the atmosphere. The nuclear force in our secret centre, this Minotaur, symbolises the good or the evil of which we are capable. In this sense, it is a place of naked desires, and while many will mercifully never find expression, all of them must undergo transformation as we mature.

The paradox and the dilemma is that our potential cannot be realised in any safe, abstract way, but only by hands-on contact, by risk and struggle. We ourselves must carry the light into the heart of our darkness or we shall be making a *de facto* option for no more growth. Light is the only solution for inner darkness. Yet to be a light-bearer, even to ourselves, is a costly exercise because it feels like death and dissolution and despair. For the Minotaur, the darkness itself, it is death, dissolution and despair. Yet the health of our society requires that there always be some people who have opened up the depths of themselves in this way. In every walk of life, it is one of the tasks of the contemplative heart to keep the collective unconscious open to the Light, a task doubly necessary in those periods of history when explicit knowledge of God is at a low ebb. As we approach the entrance to this labyrinth in our hearts, we must do what Ariadne did and seek a thread so we can find our way out. It is no help to anyone if we get lost in the maze. Clare shows us that we can enter the most dangerous places if we follow the thread of Christ, cleaving to the humanity of the Word of God. Christ, we might say, is the true Ariadne, the one who entered the cosmic maze and confronted the ultimate Minotaur. On his way out, he left a guiding thread so that we can now tread, personally, the path which Christ trod cosmically. Although Clare did not use that language, her life itself shows that she did confront her Minotaur and all her wild beasts. She set out to open herself to the light of God: 'love totally the one who gave himself totally for your love', was the way she put it, and she would never have come to such inner radiance had she not deliberately and consciously faced the dark within. As we shall see, there is some evidence to suggest that this tension between light and dark was exactly the image which best expressed the fundamental polarity of her life, and that holiness, for her, came from this progressive opening of herself to the light of God.

In 1300, nearly a hundred years after Clare's flight, Dante wrote his great *Divina Commedia*, telling of the time when he too was in a dark and difficult wood, his heart shaken by doubts and dangers. Shafts of light were few, the sun far, far off. His progress was barred by wild beasts of unprecedented ferocity, the Minotaur in Renaissance clothing. Virgil, his soul's tutor, said that since Dante was afraid to confront these wild beasts then he, Virgil, had been sent to lead him to Paradise by another route, though it would prove longer and more terrible. It was a road which passed through damnation itself, then through repentance and finally, helped by a host of others, to Paradise. It also, of course, wove the most wonderful poetry and it is arguably one of the clearest signs that we have not yet fully entered our salvation, that we still make greater poetry out of pain than out of paradise.

Dante's tale is a most appropriate allegory for today when, unable to confront our wild beasts, we too are having to tread a far more terrible path. It is a dreadful experience when, like him, we reach an impasse, unable because of wild beasts to progress to Paradise. Finally, Dante, overcome with fear, was 'reduced to nothing' (Clare's words),[2] the very condition he had been trying to avoid, the very state to which he had been convinced the wild beasts would reduce him. With Clare, on the other hand, we see that when the way was blocked she was able to summon the spiritual energy to tackle the task. In the negations of poverty, she had actually chosen freely that very nothing which Dante struggled so hard to leave behind him. In this way, she imitated Christ who, knowing it to be essential, also chose it freely, thereby laying down this thread of true humanity for us to follow. So at the moment of challenge, Clare and Dante made radically opposite decisions which affected the rest of their journeys. Dante, travelling by 'another route', circumvented and evaded the symbolic beasts but had to go through the terrible circles of hell instead. There he did not confront his wild beasts but found himself handed over to them as he experienced all the circles of hell. Clare, by confronting the wild beasts in the arena of her own heart, travelled by the most direct route of all to the inner circle of Paradise. We should note that confrontation does not guarantee an absence of painful passages. It may cost us, as we say, a leg and an arm, but there is all the difference in the world between confronting all that lies in our hearts – as Clare did, and being handed over to it – as Dante was.

Another interesting reflection which emerges from their two stories is the difference between a community and the enforced togetherness of hell – that terrible communal solitude. The modern image for this last could be an isolated flat in a tower block, every neighbour a potential enemy and no playground for children. It is a parody of community, typifying all that Clare meant when she said that this world will surely cheat us. By definition, there is no isolated solution to this isolation. To emerge from isolation, we need each other. Clare fully realised the pain and folly of isolation and knew what a gift we are to each other. 'The Lord gave me sisters' she said, just as Francis had said 'The Lord gave me brothers'. It is a sign of the Kingdom when we struggle to build community, for then the new wine of the Kingdom begins to be pressed from a bunch of grapes, namely us. When we close in on ourselves and regard others as enemies, we are reinforcing what we see all around us – structures rending and breaking apart, wild beasts barring the way like daemonic forces. Major institutions of all kinds are in crisis today because the dark wood, like a terrifying parody of the Word, is social and historical as well as personal. Like Dante, we need a guide, we need exemplars who have confronted their own violence and lived to tell the tale, we need guides we can trust. Clare entered the dark wood for precisely this, to be a co-operator with Christ who came 'for all our sakes, snatching us from the power of the prince of darkness',[3] rescuing us from the wild beasts within.

Approaching this from yet another standpoint, Clare also saw that all our affliction, crisis, *angst* and distress, which she gathered together under the word tribulation, are linked to the building of the Kingdom in the same way as pain and disorder are linked together. She realised that the death and resurrection

of Christ are one reality, stapled together by the cross. She never
said that suffering is a punishment for our sinfulness, nor that
we must suffer to carve out spaces for joy in ourselves. She only
insisted that Christ has moved right to the boundaries of our
negative experiences in order to fill them with the creative
presence of our blissful God. The purpose of our journey
through that labyrinth is to initiate us into the whole complexus
of Christ's experience. Now there is no part of our being outside
redemption, nowhere too distant for pain to be transmuted
into joy. Thinking about this interplay of loss and enrichment,
pain and bliss, she writes a little song about this true poverty,
this readiness to rediscover the negative as the bearer of joy:

> O blessed poverty,
> who gives to those who love and choose her
> eternal riches;
> O holy poverty,
> to those who hold and long for her
> God has promised the kingdom of heaven
> and has certainly granted
> eternal glory and blessed life!
> O faithful poverty:
> the Lord Jesus Christ,
> who ruled heaven and earth and still does,
> he who also spoke and things were made,
> chose to embrace you before all else![4]

As we search for we know not what, we often blunder into
the dark wood without realising it, calling it by other names.
Because Christ has made himself one of us, his threat lies there
for anyone to use, even though we do not know him or know
that his are the footprints we track. One day we shall find, if we
continue to pursue this spoor, that the lion we seek is the Lion
of Judah, that we and God had been in close relationship long
before we knew we had even begun to seek God. We shall be
amazed at our unexpected salvation, astonished to find that
even our mistakes were hit and run raids on life in abundance.
Did not the Lord himself say that the Kingdom must be taken
by storm? Later still, we shall find that life in abundance falls
into our palm like a ripe apple, for it is a gift to an empty hand.
In that way, God becomes intimate with us, and many wild beasts
are conquered simply by that presence. To approach God is

itself liberation, and no matter how deep our hunger or tortured our *angst,* God is deep too, Christ also tortured.

4

A Nut Beneath the Hammer

❖

Let us go to him outside the camp and share his degradation. *

Among the brothers who came to meet Clare, on that night when she arrived at the Porziuncola, was her cousin Rufino, who may well have been instrumental in bringing her to Francis in the first place. Rufino was a shy, quiet man who found preaching very difficult. Francis had told him to go and preach in Assisi one day and, when Rufino begged to be let off, punished his lack of obedience by insisting that he took off his habit and went wearing nothing but his breeches. Rufino was much laughed at as he entered the Cathedral pulpit. Meanwhile, Francis had been overcome with remorse. Rufino, he reflected, is one of the foremost gentlemen of Assisi – what a way to treat him! So he immediately took off his own habit and he too went to Assisi wearing only his breeches, followed by the faithful Leo, discreetly carrying two habits. Francis found Rufino preaching with immense fervour and joined him in the pulpit where the two of them so touched the hearts of those present that many lives were changed that day. Then they both put on their habits and returned to St Mary of the Angels praising God.

Scholars think this story belongs to the very early days. In that case, it must have taken considerable courage for Clare to commit herself to Francis' guidance. Fortunately, he dealt with her quite differently, firing her with love for God, giving scope to her latent capacity for love, leaving her free to tackle problems in her own way and make her own decisions. During their meetings, his words fired her because what he said confirmed what was already in her heart. His words, struck from the furnace of his prayer, rang true to her own prayer, in a way which they both realised was no stray chance but a sharing in the burning desires of Christ. Clare comes across to us as full of

---

* Hebrews 13:13.

eagerness, wholly free from the sort of cynicism which leaves us spiritually tired. She was ready for further confrontation with wild beasts, ready to tackle the sin which she recognised in her own heart. The Baal Shem Tov, joyful initiator of the Hasidic movement in Judaism, used to say that we never see sin, we only ever recognise it. 'Sinners are mirrors; when we see faults in them, we must realise that they only reflect the evil in us.' The truly holy see no evil because they have none. Once again we find evil acting as a parody of good, even to being a mirror, this time of our hidden potential for sin. Good people, on the other hand, reflect back to us our own hidden potential for good.

Clare was already showing signs of a simplicity like that of the Baal Shem. She was already aware of the darkness within herself and understood that in order fully to follow Christ, she must travel with him through degradation and shame. We are all, sooner or later, brought to acknowledge those things in ourselves of which we are ashamed, simply in order to bring them into the light. By this honesty, Clare was to come in the end to such inner clarity that if she saw sin at all, she only saw it as Christ does, as terrible wounds in us, rendings of the wild beasts. By the generosity of her self-giving she would cut right through all compromise in the process of becoming what she was called to be: a mirror for us. She was not an anti-mirror like the Baal Shem's sinners, but a pattern for us as we, in our turn, struggle through dark woods on our journey to the light.

However, no matter how spiritually exalted Clare may have been when she came to St Mary of the Angels, she must also have been dead tired, because ordinary life goes relentlessly on. We hope she was given food and drink, although there is no mention of such a thing, but she was given what she must have needed every bit as much, warmth, encouragement and friendly love. The brothers, who had been praying and waiting, came out to greet her on a crest of exultation, with blazing torches, laughter and delight. Less than twenty-four hours before, she had been at the Palm Sunday Mass, when it was the custom then to baptise catechumens. For her, too, it had been a day of beginnings, the start of a new life in Christ. Rather as Christ had ridden triumphantly into Jerusalem, so she had gone in her finest clothes, perhaps the red dress made famous by Giotto, as a sign of the temporal glory to which she was saying farewell. The Bishop Guido had come to her place in the Cathedral of

San Rufino and handed her a palm as a sign of the cross, the goal of her endeavour. Then she had embarked on her long sharing in the passion of Christ by literally acting out the summons of the letter to the Hebrews: let us go to him outside the camp and share his degradation (Hebrews 13:14). This was the beginning of her identification with Christ.

Now, in the tiny church of St Mary of the Angels, Francis himself cut off her hair; he gave her the tonsure, say the sources, as a sign of penance. It is not clear whether Clare took religious vows by this act. She says in her Rule that she promised obedience together with her sisters, which suggests a later ceremony. Her biographer simply says that at the Porziuncola she received the insignia of holy penance and was 'married to Christ'.[1] The right to witness an act of dedication, still more of profession, was normally reserved to bishops, especially in the case of noble young ladies. As far as we know, Francis had no authority to do so – although the fact that the Bishop had come personally to Clare's pew in the Cathedral that morning, is sometimes taken, with Franciscan optimism, to imply that he knew about the plans and was indicating approval. Nevertheless, Bishop Guido was a very canny operator and it is far more likely that he bided his time. Even if he had given Clare his verbal approval, which is far from certain, he would not want to force a quarrel with the family. No amount of episcopal approval could disguise the fact that she was making a scandalous option in the strict meaning of 'scandalous', the root of which is to do with tearing or cutting asunder.

What is clear is that she regarded the tonsure as a precious and incontrovertible sign that she was now God's, and we shall see that her family also understood it as such. The legal niceties of religious profession, which could be sorted out later, interested her less than her belonging to God. This was when she began to do penance and began a lifetime of contrition – of sharing in Christ's sorrow at sin. We are told that when others sinned, she wept [2:10], and we know that she also wept at her own sin. In the end, contrition teaches us how to see as Christ sees. Beginning to do penance means stepping out along this way and placing our feet in Christ's footprints, wherever they may go. Clare's biographer says that, by this tonsure, she gave her society a bill of divorce. She also embarked on a life of downward mobility, against all the tides and currents of her upbringing, in solidarity with her new insights into the Incarnation of Christ. In her own life, she was to become a true incarnation of the Incarnation, a mirror to the world of our generous God who is truly poor because so truly generous.

From St Mary of the Angels, Francis and the brothers led her to the Benedictine Monastery of San Paolo which enjoyed extensive rights of sanctuary. There, it seems, she did not live as a noble postulant with a great dowry, but as a penniless servant, just as Francis had done at San Verecundio. She became *vilis*, one of the *vilitas*, someone of small value (paltry and trifling says the dictionary), contemptible and of no importance, the very opposite of her previous situation of honoured *nobilitas*. She and the brothers decided that she would stay at San Paolo 'until the Most High provided another place', and it says a great deal for the San Paolo community that they took in this well-known fugitive, brought to them by several notorious young men, perhaps at two or three in the morning. Like the bishop, though, the nuns were cautious; they sheltered Clare as was her right, but avoided any confrontation with her powerful family – to whom some of the nuns would probably have been related. So although they seem to have made no difficulty about receiving her, there is also no record that they did anything to protect her when the angry uncles came along. No majestic Abbess affirmed the rights of sanctuary on her behalf, even though these rights, extended by the papacy eleven years before, were a jealously defended privilege and were normally enforced by a standing army kept for the purpose. There was no sign of an army on this occasion. Clare was beginning to experience what it is like to be powerless and unimportant, to have no clout in a world where might is right. It was a dramatic and powerful lesson in the reality of Christ's decision to become despised and of no account (Isaiah 53:3), to become the one who was truly *vilis*.

With her mind fully absorbed in Christ who emptied himself of glory and became what we are, Clare set out to enter deeply into every experience which presented itself to her. She became a student of the Incarnation. Everything was a lesson in the skill of doing what Christ did. We would very much like to know more details about this interlude, especially when we recall her home life. Did she know how to work, to cook, to clean, we wonder; how real was her service, or did the nuns let her do as

she liked, hoping she would soon go away? All we know of Clare
suggests that she would not have accepted any pretence or have
settled for a token service. Entering the service of Jesus Christ
was the most real thing she had ever done and having committed herself to it, she wanted to get on with it, accepting whatever
came as the gift of the day. We get the impression that she
experienced a clear, deep delight in this service, although
she must also have realised that she could not stay hidden for
long. Like the rest of us, she would sooner or later have to state
her intentions in the public forum.

This critical demand was not made of Clare until Holy Week
had reached its crisis. Was it on Good Friday itself that she
experienced the truth of the words that our enemies can be
those of our own household (Micah 7:6)? Her identification
with Christ was to deepen through the discovery that her world
hated her because Christ had withdrawn her from it (John
15:19). This was, for her, a dramatic version of that moment to
which we must all come, though sometimes less dramatically. No
matter how we try to avoid it there is inevitably some moment of
division, some conflict of interests between Christ and temporal
power, some instant when choice is forced on us. Clare's family,
when they forced it upon her, were vociferous in condemning
her deeds (the selling of her inheritance, and her flight) and
her proposal (the following of Christ in poverty). She had disgraced them, they cried, supporting the inference that she was
not just 'entering a convent'. They started with coaxing and
promises, and moved on to persuasion, pressure and persist-
ence. The struggle lasted, we are told, for may days – no small
conflict. Positions hardened and negotiation became less possible. The pressure intensified, the temperature rose, violence
exploded; but she was not their daughter for nothing. Her
spirit, too, was strengthened in opposition; for her, too, issues
clarified and she became even more determined. She also began
to learn those skills of passive resistance which were to serve
her so well in other conflicts – with the Papacy, for instance,
and most agonising of all, with the brothers.

'If your heart should fail you' runs the old sword rune 'do
not put your trust in me' – but she had no need of swords; the
Word of God in her heart was to prove the keenest sword in
the family and it did not fail her. She kept her eyes on Christ,
certain that he was calling her to this form of poverty and

physical hardship.[2] This heart would not fail its sword. It was, and is, essential that this particular spiritual battle be fought in terms of non-violence, no matter how violent the opposition. Otherwise the violence in her heart, or our hearts, would have been a Trojan horse for the family, an enemy within fighting on their side. As these days of conflict continued, Clare learnt a great deal about the chain reactions of violence, and how aggression in ourselves is released by aggression in others, and it seems that in time she uprooted all violence from her heart until that of others had no power against her. As the Baal Shem said, we recognise violence because it is alive within us. We see without what we are within and the sin we see around us is undeniable evidence that we ourselves are sinners. If we were sinless, we would see no sin, though we might see wounds. If we were sinless, evil would have no part in us, no confederate within our camp. If we were sinless, while evil might damage the body of flesh, it would still leave our essential being pregnant with resurrection because the integrated heart cannot be touched by any violence; but such battles are not won in a single skirmish. The fact that so many of Clare's sisters spoke of her gentleness and serenity, strongly suggests that these were not just gifts of nature but the result of hard work. However remarkable she became, Clare is always one of us.

This taming of her energies began at San Paolo. There her resolve was tested and the quality of her spirit probed, she learnt to maintain peace and to tap her inner strength. She needed these lessons. She would not have been human had she not found some value for herself in being valued by her family; this is something which, however unconsciously, we all do. Being loved in childhood is part of what families are for. Those who have not had such love often have terrible struggles until they can accept that nothing can put the clock back, that what has been missed cannot be made up, that there will be healing and new life but only out of reality, not out of fantasy or substitution. Clare was two or three years beyond the normal age of marriage, having refused all suitors, so this may not have been the first time she had come into conflict with her uncles, but as far as we know it was her first experience of overt, violent personal hostility. Her buoyant recovery speaks well for her psychological toughness and basic inner security. She was at home with herself, she did not easily fall victim to self-pity but had learnt that

God can transform everything into energy. Like the sun, she was ready to leap into the noonday sky of God.

Francis, who also experienced opposition from his family and suffered greatly from it, gave its effects much thought and saw two points to be noted. One is that those who dislike or oppose us, reveal aspects of ourselves to ourselves which we do not always like and which we prefer to deny. The other follows from this, that if we are sincere in seeking God, then we will at least try to be grateful for the insight given us. Opposition is a great winnower, beating out the self-serving chaff from the grain of our dedication, ruthlessly revealing our dislike at being shown our faults. Clare came out of such tests well; her eyes were fixed beyond herself, on the figure outside the camp whom she had come to join. Yet she learnt a lot from this experience, and when the family later attacked her sister Catherine, her grasp of the issues was far clearer and more immediate, her innate authority and control much more finely tuned. She now knew much more about the workings of violence and had found what we all find, that the unresolved Minotaur in our hearts has horns, like a dilemma, on which we toss miserably.

Her endurance became a sign to her of God's holy working, a sign of that peace which is nothing to do with the absence of conflict. This peace, she said later, is our greatest stronghold, and if we endure conflict from within this stronghold, then we are unquestionably being sustained by God. She warns us against letting ourselves become angry or disturbed when others do wrong because, if we do, love will die in us.[3] She took the view that when we become upset, it is because we choose to be so, revealing that, whatever we may say, love and peace are not yet our primary values. She gives us basic guidelines about how to behave when someone acts wrongly, making it quite clear that our first task is damage limitation: we should not add to the disruption by talking about it. Our second task is to work for repair, which means forgiveness and reconciliation. In the events at San Paolo we see the foundations of this teaching being laid; we see that the more the uncles shouted, the quieter and stronger Clare became, until in time, the family's might and force blew itself out against this stronghold of her inner peace.

Rabbi Izaac Luria, a sixteenth-century Jewish master of the spiritual life, used to tell his disciples that they were like nuts with an outer shell and an inner kernel. Life hammers at the

husk but there is no other way to release the kernel. Hammered
by her family, Clare must have feared, as we all do on occasion,
that the kernel would be smashed as well as the shell. In the
end, her husk broken wide open, she came to Christ in shared
vulnerability. They were made one in degradation. She clung
to the altar cloth, we are told; and the folly of so useless a
material protection pierces our hearts, although it was a powerfully protective symbol in the spiritual sphere she was choosing
to make her own. Finally, she pulled off her veil and showed
her shorn head. The sudden sight of a shaven head can be
quite shocking, a strong symbol in its own right. Certainly her
family understood it to mean that in spite of them, she had
performed an irreversible act, made an irrevocable commitment. From now on, she was saying, her spirit would draw water
from her own well. She had escaped from bondage, surmounted
opposition and entered the service of Jesus Christ. The young
woman who will celebrate Whitsun in San Damiano will be very
different from the young girl in San Rufino Cathedral on Palm
Sunday.

Beatrice, another sister, tells us that Clare was escorted by
Francis, Bernard the lawyer and Filippo, who may have been a
priest, to the Church of Sant'Angelo in Panzo. This was not
a monastery but another Beguine-type group, living just down
the slope from the Carceri where Francis loved to go and pray.
There she remained for about a fortnight, praying and resting,
growing in understanding, clarifying the nature of her call.
These little breathing spaces are often given us, though we do
not always recognise them for what they are. During this one,
Clare moved into Easter week in every sense. It was the time
for resurrection and new beginnings. She was like the women
at the tomb early on the Sunday morning, learning lessons in
waiting, an attitude of heart which she would later extend to
considerable mystical heights. She also asked for something, a
much desired gift for herself: that her sister Catherine might
join her, that they might rediscover in the service of God the
precious closeness they had known in the old days.[4] She was
finding that it is a particularly keen pain when our journey to
God is not shared by those we most love, that it seems all wrong
when our search for love leads us away from the communion
we have already found.

Her prayer was heard and granted. Sixteen days after her

own conversion, probably on the Monday of Low week when the newly baptised set aside their white garments and begin ordinary Christian living, Catherine joined Clare at Sant'Angelo. The Lord was giving her a sister. The next day twelve angry men arrived and tried to lure her home. We cannot help wondering about the family dynamics in the Palazzo Offreduccio; what were they thinking of that they sent twelve men against two young girls? What were they expecting? Not only that, but it is disquieting to see how easily the men resorted to physical violence when Catherine refused to come home. Throughout her life Catherine showed the psychological characteristics of the younger sister; she was never quite as forceful as Clare and far more open to being bullied. One of the knights, we are told, grabbed her by the hair and tried to drag her out, striking her and kicking her meanwhile. The others joined in, trying to pick her up and bear her off. 'As if she had been attacked by lions, the young girl cried out: help me!' and they dragged her off down the slope, ripping her clothes and 'strewing the path with the hair they had torn out'.[5]

Clare was resolute in not meeting violence with anger and further violence. Physically it would have been useless, but even emotionally she did not waste her energies on argument, but instead threw them into prayer, begging God to protect his own. In answer, Catherine's body became so heavy that all the twelve men together were unable to lift it from the earth. Her uncle Monaldo was so wild with anger that he had what might have been a slight stroke, for when he raised his hand to 'strike her a lethal blow' his arm became paralysed and the pain of it afflicted him for a long time afterwards.[6] Clare then came forward. The men had already been worsted by Clare once, and it seems that she had not lost her moral ascendancy, for she asked them, with courtesy and self-possession, to entrust Catherine to her care. They gave in, going away bitterly and angrily. Catherine, who had been lying half-dead, joyfully got up and 'gave herself perpetually to the divine service'. Presently Francis came along, gave her the tonsure too, and named her Agnes, in honour of the Agnus Dei, the Lamb of God, victim for the world. It is interesting that Francis took no part in the family conflict. He may have considered Clare well able to manage, or he may have been uncertain about how she would manage. In her Testament she suggests that this was a bit of a test for her in Francis' eyes, a kind of crash-course novitiate, for she says that when he saw that she did not shrink from deprivation, poverty, hard work, distress, shame or contempt, then he welcomed her, promising to give her the same care and solicitude as he gave to his brothers. The implication is that he was waiting to see how real her aspirations were, whether she would surmount genuine opposition and stay the course.

Clare now experienced something which comes to all of us who journey forth with God, namely that the story escapes from our control. She, so clear and decisive, was now to be challenged by something even harder, a period of uncertainty and indecision. Having got what she wanted, she did not know what to do with it. She knew no peace, she was filled with uneasiness and confusion. She hardly knew herself what she was waiting for, but knew that her present situation was not the goal of her journey. After so definite a rite of passage, it would have been very unusual had she experienced no backlash, no sense of anticlimax, no uncertainties about the future. She has given us an example in overcoming both actual and symbolic obstacles: the sleeping house, the barricaded door, the inherited assumptions, the dark wood, the lack of support, the violent family. Now we look into her mirror and see ourselves in her hesitation and uncertainty as well. If we knew the will of God, we would do it, but what is it? If it matters so much, why is it so obscure? At such a time, we can only do what Clare did, wait like beggars, true mendicants of the spirit, asking for our needs and entrusting the future and the present to the architect of our labyrinth. 'Come apart and rest awhile' said Jesus to his disciples, and who are we to say we would rather get on with the work?

—— PART 2 ——
Contrition

❖

Contrition is that long, slow process by which we are granted an insight into the heart of Christ himself. By contrition, we are led from sorrowing with Christ to that suffering with Christ which springs from compassion. This journey will take us through a radical reappraisal of our lives and confront us with the same challenges as those the Lady Poverty offered to Francis, Clare and all the early Franciscans. Avarice, Prudent Providence and Procrastination are still alive and well today, still managing to keep us back from the living God.

Here, as much as anywhere, we can look at Clare to see how this process, or progress, worked out in her life. We see her go from contrition, sorrowing with Christ, to compassion, suffering with Christ and sorrowing for all who suffer. As she journeys, we see how she is changed from brightness to brightness, reflecting the glory on the face of Christ, and we know that this all happened to her as an allegory about us. Such contrition begins with sorrow for sin and will only end when our whole vision and perception have become the vision and perception of Christ.

5

The Burning Desires of God

❖

I thought it was I who desired God, but no!
it was God who desired me.*

When Clare emerged from the dark events of San Paolo and
Sant'Angelo, she was like someone emerging from a dark forest
of the spirit. A whole new life was about to begin. She was
reborn. With that emergence, something also shifted in her
relationship with the brothers who had met her and
accompanied her to San Paolo. As far as we know, she had
no brothers by blood, though she seems to have had good
relationships with one or two male cousins. But although she
was to live her life in such a feminine environment she was
clearly the sort of woman who got along very well with men. So
it must have been a great joy to her when the Lord gave her
brothers. Although they were to cause her considerable concern
in the years ahead, she was far from immune to that mystery by
which brothers and sisters will usually stand by each other
through thick and thin.

It must also have been a great joy to the brothers to have
Clare for a sister. There is every support for the belief that they
all took their new relationships in the family of God with great
seriousness and certainly all those who met her on this night
became lifelong friends. She was a deeply reflective woman –
this is clear from her writings – one who prayed and pondered,
remembered and reflected, and very soon the brothers discovered for themselves the contribution she had to make. At
the Porziuncola, they had met her with torches and lights; now
she became a light herself and, over the years, she would touch
the dark places of their hearts with her own gentle radiance
and cast the light of her experience on their journey. She
encouraged them with her friendship and challenged them
with her simplicity and unwavering commitment to poverty.

*Abu Yazid of Bistam.

42

Having once cast her anchor at San Damiano, she was always there for them, and as time went on, and her own heart was so fiercely purged, she became even more fitted to be their guide. Later, as the Order fell into deeper trouble and greater conflict, her vision and steadfastness would become increasingly necessary to them if ever they were to have hope of finding the way back to their original vision.

In a certain sense, they never did find that way back, never did recapture that joy and devotion to poverty which had marked the beginning. While Clare was alive, she was a luminous reminder, because she always clung tenaciously to her conviction that what she and Francis had established in the beginning was the way she was meant to live until the end. From Palm Sunday 1212 to the day of her death, she kept alight the flame which the Spirit had originally lit in all their hearts. From that flame, others came to kindle or rekindle their own torches, but there were many hearts in which that particular flame died out and was lost. It is an interesting variation on the animus-anima theme, that the brothers who gave light to the young girl found that she became a radiance for them far clearer than the original light.[1] She writes about this understanding of her vocation at some depth in her Testament. She was keenly aware of her responsibility, seeing it as her task to preserve the radical and simple gospel form of life, her vocation to reflect on all that had been granted her through and with Francis. For the same reason, she would have no part in compromises, even when approved by the Pope. On one occasion, the Minister General had obtained papal approval for some relaxations in the sisters' way of life and Francis went to Rome on her behalf to have them withdrawn.[2] 'Do not absolve me from following Christ,' she said later to Gregory IX.

This was the period of the fifth Crusade and the doomed Children's Crusade, and in 1215 the Fourth Lateran Council opened and bad King John signed Magna Carta at Runnymede in England. The town of Assisi also went through an unusually crowded and eventful time. A certain citizen had been told in a dream where the long lost body of the great San Rufino lay hidden, that San Rufino who had once been Bishop of Assisi and was now its most powerful patron. The Cathedral, where Clare, Francis and Frederick II had all been baptised, was dedicated in his honour. This revelation of the body of the saint was followed up and consolidated by cast-iron miracles.

Meanwhile, the Lord sent sisters to join Clare, drawn from her family and close friends. Catherine, now Agnes, was followed by another sister Beatrice, and their mother Ortolana, as well as Balvina and Amata, two nieces, and Filippa whom Clare had probably met as a child in exile in Perugia. Her mother's pilgrimage companion, Pacifica, came and Christiana who had been in the Palazzo Offreduccio the night Clare escaped, and several others. Francis too was busy, setting out in 1212 for Compostella with Brother Bernard, but he fell ill and came home. In 1216, the dying Innocent III made the final provision in his imaginative and far-sighted policy about new religious groups (a policy which more or less died with him) by confirming the Privilege of Poverty for Clare. This allowed Clare to live by trust in God, and exempted her and the community from the Council's ruling that convents and monasteries must be on a sound financial footing and hold property in common. This also suggests that Clare's community may not have been seen, at that date, as part of an existing Order. It may also explain why she was later put under pressure to affiliate with the Benedictines. In practice, it meant that she had won a round in her lifelong battle for poverty. She had also begun her lifelong apprenticeship in dealing with the system and had embarked on trying to express the working of the Spirit of the Lord in a language which the institutional Church could integrate.

In 1221 Peter Catani, one of the very early brothers, died, the first of them to do so. These were also the years when Francis was writing his Rule. In 1224, he received the Stigmata, the marks of Christ's wounds in his own body, and Clare fell seriously ill, as if the tornado of love which nearly swept him out of the world swirled around her body too. Later, Francis came to stay in a little hut near San Damiano. She made him soft moccasins for his wounded feet and he wrote the Canticle of Creation, reconciling the Podestà and the Bishop, honouring Sister Death as he felt her approach, and perhaps even honouring Clare herself in the subtle play on her name which he wove into the work. 'Our sister Moon and the stars,' he sang, 'which God has created clear (*claras*) precious and beautiful.' Without doubt Clare had been for him a clear light in dark places, a precious person, beautiful in every way.

Two years later he was dead and her life crossed the second of its major watersheds. The following year was also marked by a terrible famine, which must have meant near starvation for her community, living on alms as they did. The year after that, Francis was canonised. There also took place an unrelated event which, if she knew about it, would have held some significance for her. This was the approval, in spite of all the Council had said about no new rules, of the Carmelite Rule (written before the Council). In that same year, too, the Bishop of Assisi who had covered Francis with his cloak, who had given Clare her palm at that Palm Sunday Mass and had allowed her to live at San Damiano, the bishop who had quarrelled with the mayor (whose daughter was in Clare's community) and who had been reconciled by Francis, this Bishop of Assisi, Guido, also died. This was in 1228. The ties with the beginning were becoming frayed.

These were some of the external events which formed the context of Clare's inner journey, a journey which was both independent of outer events and moulded by them. Events were soon to demand that she put what she had learnt into words, so that others (and we) could benefit from it. In Prague, in 1234, the 23-year-old Agnes, Princess of Bohemia, was wanting to establish and live this form of life which she had heard about from the brothers in Bohemia, who probably also took news of Agnes back to Clare. We know from a letter which Gregory IX wrote to Blanche of Castile on 11 June 1234, that Clare sent the younger woman four small gifts: a wooden cross, an earthenware bowl, a monastic veil and some prayer beads. In her accompanying letter, Clare sent out the fundamental elements of the service of Jesus Christ, as she herself understood it. As we become more familiar with the format and structure of the medieval letter, the development of Clare's thought becomes much clearer to us. Her letters are densely packed with thoughts, and constructed in a way quite different from ours today. They are more like a piece of architecture than a casual communication to a friend, and this must always be borne in mind. The bonus is that we can scrutinise her words, constructions and parallels with a reasonable confidence that she did indeed mean the things we are reading into them.

In this letter to Agnes, Clare picks up echoes of some words from Isaiah in which God speaks about the restored kingdom:

For now I create a new heaven and a new earth, and the past will
not be remembered and will come no more to men's minds. Be
glad and rejoice for ever and ever for what I am creating, because
now I create Jerusalem 'Joy' and her people 'Gladness'. I shall
rejoice over Jerusalem and exult in my people. (65:17–19)

She tells Agnes that she, Clare, also is glad and rejoicing greatly;
I exult, she says, at the reports I am hearing about you. Agnes
was making a clear option for the new creation, for joy and
gladness. She was choosing, as Clare puts it, to 'do' or 'make'
the service of Jesus Christ, a service which itself is the true
Jerusalem. Agnes is engaged on a 'praiseworthy piece of commerce', an exchange by which she barters transient glory for
the heart of things. Even the greatness of the particular transient glory which Agnes is surrendering (or offering) will be
surpassed by the gift of God to be given in return. By yielding
a hollow glory in exchange for the heart of the universe, Agnes
is in every way a winner.

In this letter, Clare develops her insights about Christ. She
understands that Christ is not simply 'more'. He is, in today's
phrase, something else; in Clare's words, he is a bridegroom of
a far greater *kind* of nobility. In the Middle Ages, nobility itself
was held to be a gift from God, presumably because life was so
much more pleasant for the nobility than for the poor, but
Clare, as always, has her own slant on this. Pushing words to
their limits, she turns the whole concept of nobility on its head
by saying that true nobility is found on the cross with Christ,
through poverty and physical hardship.

With your whole being and all your heart, you have preferred most
holy poverty and physical hardship, you have taken to yourself the
Lord Jesus Christ, a Bridegroom of a far greater kind of nobility.
    Therefore be strengthened, my dearest sister – or rather, Lady
greatly respected – for you are the beloved, the mother and the
sister of my Lord Jesus Christ. You are now most splendidly distin-
guished by the insignia of inviolable virginity and most holy poverty
– so be strengthened in the holy service which has been begun by
the burning longing of the poor crucified one.[3]

It is the poor and crucified one who is truly great, and the
poverty and hardship of this lord's service is the true meaning
of glory. To do his service means to do his will, and it is this –
as the Lord himself said – which makes us his mother, sister or

brother, and beloved, and there is no greater glory than that. Having entered this service and begun to learn the skills of self-giving, we also begin to experience for ourselves what it means to say that Christ, Son of the Most High, is a Lord of a far greater kind of nobility. Though he was so great a Lord, he chose to embrace poverty to the extent that he had nowhere to lay his head. So, she goes on, stringing scripture together in a characteristic manner, he bowed his head and gave up the spirit.

Beyond that again, however, lies a further insight. This service of Jesus Christ is not simply a service which we enter but a service which he himself is continually performing for the human race. Christ is the true servant who neither wavers nor is crushed. All through his life, he worked for true justice on this earth and will continue to work until it is established. 'My Father goes on working,' said Jesus (John 5:18), 'and so do I.' At his ascension he left us another like himself, the Spirit, who is still at work in our hearts with 'God's holy manner of working' and we, too, when we work, do so by the grace of God (Isaiah 42:1–4). Clare was very conscious of God's working and our participation in that work. She speaks in her Rule about the sisters to whom the Lord has given the grace of working,[4] and she means – the work or service of Jesus Christ, which takes all sorts of mundane and practical forms. The span of Clare's thought, like the span of God's work, runs from creation to the washing up. Nothing is too great or too small. This is the service into which we are called when we are invited to share in his passion and death for the redemption of all. This is what doing a service to Jesus Christ means, and in a single, powerful sentence, Clare links our service with the burning longings of Christ:

> Be strengthened in the holy service which has been begun by the burning longing of the poor crucified one.[5]

She came to this insight by her usual, profoundly incarnational, route, that is, she reflected on the facts. Where did the Franciscan story begin unless in the chapel of San Damiano? The three companions tell us what happened:

> While Francis was walking near the church of San Damiano, an inner voice bade him go in and pray. He obeyed, and kneeling before an image of the crucified Saviour, he began to pray most devoutly. A tender, compassionate voice then spoke to him: 'Francis, do you not see that my house is falling into ruin? Go and repair it

for me. . . From that hour his heart was stricken and wounded with melting love and compassion for the passion of Christ, and for the rest of his life he carried in it the wounds of the Lord Jesus.[6]

He had entered the service of Jesus Christ, called into it by the burning longing of the crucified for him to 'repair my house', and many lives were changed as a result.

This was the primary revelation for Francis and Clare. That tender, compassionate voice of the Crucified spoke about God's longing, God's passion, and Francis was stricken to the heart, wounded with the love and compassion of Christ. The contemporary documents are full of words like burning, being ardent, being on fire, striking sparks from the furnace of their hearts; or about being cold or lukewarm. When Clare taught her sisters about prayer, she taught them always to keep in touch with that tender and compassionate heart of Christ, showing them how 'to grow warm again through the exercise of prayer, and leaving the listlessness of not caring, to commit their cold lack of devotion to the flames of holy love'.[7] The listlessness of not caring, which so easily afflicts us all, is a terrible cul-de-sac from which we make no effort to escape precisely because we have ceased to care. Clare taught her novices, and teaches us in the process, that we can throw that particular bit of rubbish into the furnace of Christ's love. As a cure, it is brilliant because it does not require us to 'snap out of it' – by definition impossible – but simply says that there is this furnace where our listlessness is like snow in the boiler room. We do not have to do anything except be near the furnace. That is the exercise: to go near the furnace, to be in the presence of the poor, crucified One. She makes no requirements of 'success' in prayer, only that we perform the exercise. Inevitably we shall grow warm if we stand near that compassionate furnace for long, and in time spontaneous combustion will take place, we will catch fire from his burning longing.

This work which engages God is one of both creating and repairing. The service becomes possible for us by invitation, an invitation into the work which Christ undertook when he came into this world. We are called to build the new Jerusalem. This demands dedication and struggle from us, but all the while it is God who is creating Jerusalem 'Joy' and the people of God, 'Gladness'. We would be very rash to entrust ourselves to our own burning longing because this changes direction at the slightest shift in the breeze of circumstances, but we can wisely, or prudently as Clare would say, commit ourselves to this service of Christ's, because the burning longing of the Lord is eternal and everlasting. The longing itself springs from the mysterious depths of the Godhead, and the burning of it is all mystery.

The first letter which Clare wrote to Agnes of Prague is devoted to this theme of exchanging one form of service for another. In it, Clare balances the transient against the enduring, well aware that while the things of time are very much with us, the Kingdom too is here and now or nowhere. Into this Kingdom, God has (already) transferred us (Colossians 1:13). Our dilemma is that although we live in the midst of both the transient and the enduring, there is something in us which finds the transient much easier to deal with. The enduring alarms us, seeming to require a dependability we know we lack. The transient leaves more margin for error and therefore for reassessment. It demands less commitment. Clare, in stressing that this service is really the Lord's work, and that our part is to be a co-operator not the top management, offers us a way forward which we can both accept and be challenged by.

There is an inner dynamism in her thought which emerges through the verbs she uses. When she speaks of 'making' or 'doing' the service of Christ, it recalls the way she speaks in her Rule of making or doing the Divine Office.[8] She is suggesting that we choose this service although it is also, mysteriously, a work of God. The service is that in Christ we have been reconciled to God, and God had 'given us the work of handing on this reconciliation' (2 Corinthians 5:18). In other words, what has happened for us can happen for others. What happened to us happened on behalf of others. We are back at the mirror theme; we have been set as a pattern for others to follow, and if we give our whole selves to this, then we will give a noble example.

The heart of all this is what Clare calls the choice of poverty. As she understands it, this is a decision to bring all we have and are into line with God's values, which are values of heart and spirit rather than power and prestige, values of giving rather than having. This is why she focuses so often on Christ in the crib and on the cross, because those were the moments when

that value system of the heart was most dramatically portrayed.
She encourages us to commit ourselves

> for love of that God who was placed poor in the crib,
> who lived poor in the world
> and who remained naked on the gibbet,[9]

and in our turn to encourage others to do the same. For Clare,
the scenes of Christ in the crib and on the cross were rather
like stills from a film, something dynamic and mobile held
motionless for a while so that we can see it better. They were
moments when Christ's inner life was fully expressed by his
outer life, and this inner–outer tension was something which
both Francis and Clare worked hard to keep in balance. Looking at these stills, they could see that those moments of poverty
were instants of total harmony and integration, something rare
in our human way of living. For the same reason, they were
moments of intense fullness, and this is the true import of a
poverty which is holy. So when Clare speaks of 'leaving the
temporal for the eternal', she is not talking about a life-denying,
other-worldly preference, but about living in such a way that
our here-and-now lives are set in the wider context of God's
work in the world. That context is the holy service to which
Christ calls us, and again Clare's concrete imagination saw it as
almost a physical place, the contemplative space. She speaks of
being 'placed' in this place, defined by the co-ordinates of crib
and cross.

The indications of this service, the insignia as she calls them,
are poverty, the hallmark of generosity, and virginity, which
Clare sees as one way of putting even our mortal bodies at the
service of the enduring. A woman of her time, she places more
value on virginity than we might, but typically, she also leaves
the concept and the reality much enriched – even for us.
Nowhere does she suggest that virginity is a prerequisite for
holiness; on the contrary, as we have seen, she was influential
in the spiritual lives of an enormous number of people, married
and single, men and women. In her thinking, virginity is less a
matter of what we have not done and more a matter of what
we shall become. When you have accepted Christ, she tells
Agnes, then you will be a virgin, that is, you will be made
whole.

> Loving him, you are chaste,
> touching him, you are made pure,
> taking him to yourself, you are a virgin.[10]

Virginity is a sign and a gift, not a missed opportunity or the fruit of denial. It compares with physical virginity rather, she hints, as Frederick II compares with Christ! The two are generically different. Just as Christ has a different kind of nobility, so he is a different kind of Bridegroom. He is not simply greater but qualitatively other. As a result, the kind of fruitfulness which comes from union with Christ is also other. In fact it is altogether new, so there is nothing to be gained by comparing it with our more familiar earthly realities. In this new situation, virginity follows upon fruitfulness, it is the fruit of fruitfulness rather than that which must be given away in the cause of fruitfulness. When Clare's sisters stress, as they often do, her lifelong virginity (and slightly shock us by seeming to regard it as remarkable), this is part of what they are meaning. She showed forth, even in her body, what it means to live in the Kingdom. Into that same Kingdom, however, we are all invited. It is the new heaven and the new earth where Jerusalem is joy and the people are gladness itself. It is participation in the creativity of God.

6

Echoes of Paradise

❖

Run with love, run with patience.*

When we try to get a picture of Clare's life as a whole, we see that it has an oscillating, twofold movement which, on further thought, we may recognise. Her energy runs outward to action and inward to reflection, each part of the movement drawing on the previous one and preparing for the next. We have already seen how she was stirred by the call of God and how this drove her, like Christ himself, out into the relative wilderness of a break with her past. From this grew a new beginning, so the energy ran inward again toward the centre as she and Agnes found their feet at San Damiano. Then a community began to gather and Clare's influence spread further afield. Yet she herself remained faithful to the inner source of her energy which then led her on to other challenges, such as the extraordinary expansion of her way of life, or the insights about Islam brought to her from the East by Francis. So the inner deepening and the outer extension developed together. As her roots sank deeper, so her branches spread wider.

The connecting thread of this twofold movement was the lesson she had learnt from Francis, that Christ was her Way to God.

> The Son of God became the way for us, which by word and example our most blessed father Francis showed us and taught us, being himself a true lover and imitator.[1]

'Christ is the Way, and Francis showed it to me.' This is our first lesson in Clare's school, as essential to contemplative prayer as the letters of the alphabet to literature. From Francis, she learnt the single eye which the Gospel recommends, she learnt to see the love of God summed up in Christ, and she learnt to

---

*Sacrum Commercium, 67 (Omnibus p. 1595).

52

express her own response through poverty and simplicity. From Francis, she learnt how to read the Gospel and put it into practice. Initially, they chose to be poor because Christ had done so by becoming man and they longed to respond with an equally improvident generosity. Then they found that the more they identified with Christ in his self-emptying, the more the inner, spiritual heart of poverty was revealed. Trying to live as Christ had lived, they began to see as Christ sees and to discover new depths in that exchange by which Christ, while remaining what he was, became what he was not.[2] They also began to learn about the other half of that cyclic movement in which we, through the straitened circumstances of Christ in his poverty, are led back to the heart of the Godhead.

This oscillation between action and reflection was also at work in the larger group of Franciscans. So we find in 1227, soon after Francis' death, that an unknown Franciscan reflected on the issues raised by poverty in an allegorical study called the *Holy Exchange of Saint Francis and the Lady Poverty*. We have already glanced at Clare's later comments on this theme of exchange, and now we come to a treatment of it from one of the men in the Order. The work is an extended allegory about Francis' search for this elusive Lady Poverty and his various trials as he searches for her, and how he finally discovers her on an isolated mountaintop. She is far from welcoming, shouting advice and taunts down the mountain to him and testing his resolution by putting him through what amounts to a novitiate. Even her taunts, however, later turn out to spring from a deep insight into the knots and twists of human nature, and she gives him (and us) some sound advice.

Observing the process by which she tests Francis' heart, we learn a great deal about the deceptions we practise on ourselves. She reveals the way we promise far more than we can deliver so that we are bound to fail, enabling us then to give up and sink back into the mud with relief. She reveals the parody of humility in our arrogant assumption that we have a right to God's special protection just because we are weak. There is all the difference in the world, she says, between trusting in God, and assuming that God will rescue us from disasters of our own making. Most of us imagine that because we now rely on grace everything will be easy, but all we have really learnt is the acceptable language. Major obstacles still remain between us and God;

we still have little understanding of our essential destitution. We still deny that our house is built on sand, even when we make it manifest by our false sense of security, shown by our casual laziness and ready excuses. We still put things off: tomorrow, tomorrow, tomorrow. While we often fool ourselves, however, we fail to fool the Lady Poverty who has seen it all before. I know all about the human heart, she says, in a medieval version of 'I was not born yesterday'.

To cut through such twists of self-deception, we need her uncompromising insights; otherwise all our paths will lead us to disaster. We can draw endless strength from her because she draws infinite strength from Christ, the one who is faithful and true. Cleaving fast to him, she learnt to be faithful just as he was faithful on the cross, and like him she learnt fidelity in order to teach it to us. Because she has nothing to lose, she is free to be faithful, and when we have no hidden agendas or vested interests, then we too will be capable of fidelity and freedom. We see here the difference between worldly wisdom and God's wisdom. Worldly wisdom offers escapes, God's wisdom invites us into a new country and leads us to this truth: that most of the things we call essential are not so. They are false gods. Their only likeness to God is that they share their essence with us, in their case their emptiness, while God shares the fullness of the divine nature hidden in Christ.

In a world where there is a poverty which is obviously bad, unjust and exploitative, the Lady Poverty stands for totally self-giving generosity, and indicates that the solution to this negative form of poverty is not that we all become rich, but that we all become generous. This would be a sign that the poor and generous Christ was with us. When we are poor and deprived, in need and destitute, the Lady Poverty comes to join us just as she joined Christ and walked with him from the crib to the cross. She personifies loving discipleship. If we can welcome her through our experience of loss, then we are accepting reality, and change will inevitably follow such an acceptance. Things may well get worse, but they will not remain the same. It is part of our dilemma that while we can never force growth, we can prevent it, and we often do so simply by denying the reality which presents itself to us.

Clare tells us that in the difficult time after Francis died, she experienced some of this for herself, being made painfully aware of her fragility and learning to fear it. It seems that she had never been really stretched until then, but had always found the resources for any challenge. This time she felt tested far beyond her strength. Francis who was her strength, was now her loss; where could she draw strength to tackle the loss of strength? She alludes to this fragility in her Testament:

> I, Clare, considering this most high profession of ours, and the command of such a father, and the fragility of others – which we feared in ourselves after the death of our holy father Francis, our pillar and sole consolation after God – again and again freely committed us to our Lady most holy Poverty.[3]

This was a way of saying that in her loss, she chose freely what had become inevitable, loss itself. She ceased (or tried to cease) struggling, allowing reality to flow again, trusting that the river would eventually run into the sea of God. The service of God offers us no guarantee against pain, rather the contrary, but the promise of abundant life as a sure guarantee against everlasting death. To turn death into life is part of the alchemy of God, and the Lady Poverty is the apprentice of that alchemy.

The Lady Poverty told Francis that left to ourselves we are inveterate collectors and that most of our collection is foolishness and false values. Helped by her, though, we may learn some sense and even, with luck, some wisdom, she says! Francis meekly replies that he and his brothers are well aware that they need her, and the bare mountaintop has become a symbol to them of their difficult climb out of the addictions of human nature. On the mountaintop, they had found the thin, cold air and the infinite view that they desired. In acknowledgement of their right thinking, she begins to tell them her story, how she and Adam (no mention of Eve) had lived together in paradise, how she had assumed it would be forever and how revolted she had been to find Adam 'clothed in the skins of the dead' and so had left him.

> 'From that time I did not find where to rest my foot . . . and all the while the Cherubim stood before the gate of Paradise with a flaming sword . . . until the Most High came into the world from the bosom of his father, and sought me out most graciously.'

Now she can and will show them the way back to that lost Paradise.

In some measure, it was an important key idea for Clare and the early Franciscans that simplicity and poverty restore us to Paradise. They are signs in our hearts that God is at work restoring harmony, calming our clamorous desires. True poverty of spirit, says Clare, is blessed, holy and faithful, and God gives life to those who long for her.[4] We strengthen this life in ourselves when we try to contain our greed a little, or to simplify our demands, or to leave behind our fear and selfishness, for all these cover us like dodder on a gorse bush which forms a tight net of fine threads that slowly strangle the plant beneath. If we follow Clare's advice, we will come to see that poverty is not primarily concerned with economics but with the heart. It is freedom from the treadmill of self-centredness. It is because they were free in this way that Francis and Clare are so attractive to us. They have about them that for which we long. They are like citizens and we in exile, and, like many exiles, we labour under a weight of inertia almost too great for our longings to sweep us home.

Freedom of spirit is a sign which we all understand, a clear indication that here is someone on the way to the Kingdom. Freedom is the language of the Kingdom because it means we are ready to hear the Word of God and keep it, and then we are like Isaiah who found that the more he listened to God, the more God seemed to be speaking to him. 'Each morning he wakes me to hear, to listen like a disciple. . . and I made no resistance, neither did I turn away' (Isaiah 50:4,5). It is keeping the Word of God which makes us free, a paradox incomprehensible to our libertarian culture. Francis pointed out that Adam could have eaten from any tree in Paradise (God's word to him) except one,[5] which instantly became the only one he wanted. Because he insisted on his own way, he set in motion patterns of imprisonment which we all know only too well. We are too like the churning wheels of a car, making the rut deeper for each other, generation after generation. Francis maintained that disobedience is a moral expression of something which shows itself materially as greed. In our greed, we want to have good things for ourselves and security for tomorrow, because we are not sure about the Lord. Our disobedience is that we want to be in control – the one thing for which we are not fitted, so we worry about the future, in spite of the Lord's dry comment that today usually has enough worries to be going on

with. We long to know how God is going to run things, especially
us, and we are always seduced by the chance of knowledge
about what will hit us next, what will be good and what evil.
That is like a bite taken from the fruit of the tree of knowledge.
Yet chewing that bite is so against our true nature that it instantly
becomes a poisonous fruit for us, destroying our freedom and
bringing disaster. We think of Macbeth in the inaccurate and
powerful way that Shakespeare portrayed him, ineluctably
drawn to kingship because it had been prophesied, and seeing
that as justifying all the corpses littering his way to the throne.
Our dilemma is that, while goodness is simple, badness is easy
and we want both. No wonder our spiritual technology is so
primitive when we spend our lives rediscovering the wheel; yet
any acorn knows how to roll downhill. Most of us could learn
wisdom from that acorn.

Francis and Clare understood the link between poverty and
Paradise to express the way Christ, the truly poor man, brought
us life in abundance. They also experienced for themselves that
when poverty was shared, community was discovered and that
this is the nucleus of the Kingdom. It is also the wisdom of the
acorn!

> After the Lord gave me brothers, the Most High Himself revealed
> to me that I should live according to the form of the Holy Gospel.
> And those who came to receive life gave to the poor everything
> they were capable of possessing – and we had no desire for anything
> more.[6]

This was the real sign of conversion in those early brothers, that
they had no desire for anything more. Giving everything away
was heady and liberating, an effect they were loath to lose; they
discovered for themselves that joy, the harbinger of Paradise,
springs from generosity. For them, as for us, the Lady Poverty
was like an assay mark, an authentication of simplicity.

The Lady Poverty told Francis that when Christ emptied himself to become like us,[7] she was so close to him that she hung
on the cross with him, where even his mother could not go.
'You suffered with him,' Francis replies in the allegory, 'so that
nothing in him should appear more glorious than you.'[8] Dante
(who had probably read this work and was almost certainly a
Franciscan Tertiary) said that after Christ died, Poverty was like
a widow and remained so for twelve hundred years, until Francis

sought her out. Their harmony and their union, their *dolce sguardo*,[9] their loving looks, moved many to follow Christ, because Christ and the Lady Poverty are like mirror images of each other. Pay attention, says Clare,

> to the elements of this mirror: the poverty of the one placed in a crib and wrapped in tiny garments; Oh wonderful lowliness! Oh astounding poverty! The King of Angels, the Lord of the heavens and the earth lying back in a manger. Then, in the centre of the mirror, consider the lowliness, or at least the blessed poverty, the infinite labour and effort which he endured for the redemption of the human race. Finally, deep in that same mirror, contemplate the unimaginable love, through which he chose to suffer on the Tree of the cross and, on that same Tree, to die the most disgraceful of all kinds of death.[10]

While he was searching for the Lady Poverty, Francis had met many of the wise and great of this world, and they had all assured him that they meant to make the most of their good luck and become as rich as possible while they could. Life is short, they said, and true wisdom is to look after your own. Sharing is particularly foolish when there is not enough for everyone. There is an unspoken assumption in the *Sacrum Commercium* that private property has no place in Paradise, and it drops more than a hint that wealth is the result of greed and possessiveness. This notion has led Franciscans into a certain amount of trouble over the years, but the point becomes clearer when we reverse it and remember that generosity is a sign of Paradise restored. Francis and Clare, from very different backgrounds, both understood how wealth leads to more wealth in a self-perpetuating cycle of wealth, possessiveness, greed and aggression. Obviously there are some powerful social statements underlying the analysis of our Lady Poverty; perhaps the whole allegory should be required reading for those in public office. She makes some very challenging comments about the poorer people in a society, suggesting that the vitality of religion and the way we treat the poor are a thermometer for each other. When she, Lady Poverty, is rejected (and even more so when religion is either absent or just a pious front) then people will begin to snipe at the poor, seeing them as lazy, rough, uncultured and unfeeling, as being somehow to blame for their poverty.

To help us retain a cutting edge in society, this vigorous lady gives us guidelines for living in a materialistic world, and details the forces which can tug us off course. One of the most powerful is our own greed, here called the Lady Avarice. We long most painfully for possessions when we have just enough to make riches seem possible but not enough to satisfy our desires. The sight of others with great possessions convinces us that we have as much right to ownership on a grand scale as they do – or at least a right to more than we have at present. Sometimes Avarice dresses up as discretion, warning us not to be generous with others before our own needs are met. Give away a little but keep some in hand. Cut back on what you give to those poorer than yourself and concentrate on currying favour with the mighty. There are all sorts of good reasons for this and they might even be useful in our service of God and the poor! Our dilemma is that, although this might be true, the wash of such arguments will sink us while we are still collecting our wits. It is not wise to mess about in boats like these. Clare's advice, to focus on what we have already been given, not on what we might grasp, is especially good because it returns us to our true condition of being mendicants, that is, pilgrims who wait on God's goodness. She reminds us that all the desires of our spirit find a focus in God:

> May he to whom you are devoted with all the desire of your mind deign to pour out on you the reward you long for.[11]

Another rival to Gospel poverty is called Providence (not to be confused with divine providence). Providence suggests that it is only right and sensible to make provision for ourselves and our future, though of course without overdoing it. Take what you can while you can, she says, because the opportunity may not always be there. In the far distant future, when you have enough, then you can give to the poor and devote yourself to good works, but for the moment, be careful. Agnes of Prague, because she avoided this tempting attitude, won high praise from Clare. Agnes could have married the Emperor and had an almost unlimited power to do good:

> You, more than many, could quite legitimately and with great glory, have married the illustrious Caesar – as would have been fitting to the high condition of you both – yet instead you have rejected all

that. With your whole being and with all your heart, you have preferred the most holy poverty and physical hardship.[12]

Agnes also avoided the third rival, Procrastination, the familiar habit of never getting round to it, which we may not have connected with Lady Poverty. We can always find excellent reasons for Procrastination, but often fail to recognise the cost, in terms of dwindling love and a lukewarmness which leads to an impoverished spirit. By these means, we regress from weakness of spirit to no spirit at all. This is the listlessness Clare spoke about to her novices. Not only that, but Procrastination and Avarice set up an alliance against us, so that the first encourages us to put off the day of confrontation, and Avarice persuades us to gather yet another spiritual cushion instead. We become like people afraid of enemies at the door, who fail to realise that the kind friend putting the kettle on is the greatest enemy of all. This is the stuff of dramatic irony, but its consequences in our spiritual lives can be tragic. Avarice and Procrastination, says Lady Poverty, are like Pilate and Herod, only united in doing us mischief. They teach us to long for comfort, to envy those who sensibly (as they suggest) avoid exhaustion in the spiritual struggle and to buttress ourselves against harsh reality with all kinds of warm and desirable things. In no time at all, we are back in their clutches; in fact, the Lady Poverty – who had no great opinion of human nature – said that few of us escape these deceiving ladies, and added, by way of encouragement, that most of her followers make all the mistakes in the book.

In this rather figurative way, the Lady Poverty offers a searching analysis of our condition. Clare then speaks to that condition. The allegory of poverty is for us, in several respects, like a precursor to Clare, preparing the ground for the spiritual seed which she will sow. As always, Clare speaks to us about Christ, showing how he approached these issues and how we can. Against Avarice, she places the poverty of Christ in the manger; against Providence, the poverty of Christ who lived in this world with total trust in his Father, making no provision for the morrow; against the inertia of Procrastination, she offers us the dynamic force of love shown by Christ on the cross. In her Testament, she writes:

I recommend all my sisters, those now and those who will come, that their love for that God who was placed poor in the crib, who lived poor in the world and who remained naked on the gibbet, will make the holy poverty we have promised God be observed, and that God will always encourage and preserve them in that poverty.[13]

She places all her trust in Christ's Incarnation, reassuring us that these devious characters lurking in our hearts are nothing in comparison. Christ's human life is our ground plan for idealism alone is not enough; only love made flesh in Christ will see us through thick and thin. For Clare as for Paul, Christ's love is a compelling motive. She tells us that Christ not only undertakes to beat these ladies on their own ground, that is, his resources are the stronger; but he also redefines the conflict altogether, his generosity is of a more heavenly kind, just as he is a Bridegroom of a far greater kind. We are not some battlefield where the generals fight each other over our heads. Rather we are talking about a powerful attraction: his appearance is more beautiful:

> His resources are the stronger,
> his generosity of a more heavenly kind,
> his appearance is more beautiful,
> his love more tender,
> more attractive his every grace.[14]

Tides of avarice, providence, and procrastination may come and go, will come, but will also go, but his every grace, all his graces, are *elegantior*, says Clare, once again using a rather unexpected word: they are more attractive, more exquisite, perhaps indeed more elegant, in the sense of more graceful, beautiful, subtly pleasing and more wonderful. In the end, beauty will be the deciding factor. Beauty is our surest image of the loveliness of God, it is the only truly irresistible attraction. It is beauty which draws us, beauty which is the major current in our deepest ocean.

Clearer than Light

❖

What kind of person was Clare? What was she like to live with or as an abbess? To what extent did the mature saint differ from the young girl and what was the process by which this came about? What were the inner dynamics which drove her, the inner conflicts which dogged her? A careful reading of the texts might enable us to hazard some very tentative answers. In the contemporary accounts, we see two outstanding qualities in Clare, of light and of gentleness, both of which emerged out of the all too familiar and painful struggle to grow. There are frequent references to Clare as light, playing on her name and linking it with the Latin *clara* and *claritas*, clear and clarity. There are also suggestions that her major tension was expressed in images of the dark within and her call to be 'light in the Lord'. As for her gentleness, it seems unlikely that it would have been mentioned so often had it simply been the nature of her. The stories of her early life suggest a young lady of some spirit, which supports the suspicion that her gentleness was the fruit of hard struggle.

There are two points to keep in mind here which, when we see them at work in her life, will encourage us in our own struggle. One is that maturity and holiness come to what we naturally are, because God loves the true essence of us and sees our sinfulness as a falling off from that, rather than as an expression of it (which is often our view). The second is that we mature under the hand of life itself, that daily events, especially when they are made the raw material of our prayer, work on us like wind and rain, smoothing the rough edges of our spirit. Like us, Clare must sometimes have felt that life was not smoothing her rough edges so much as eroding her out of

---

* Rune for a sundial.

all recognition. Although she said at the end of her life that since she had known Lord Jesus nothing had been too hard for her, this does not mean it had been easy. Because she went further than most of us along the road of holiness, it may have been much harder. This innately great lady could not have been transformed into the woman of invincible tenderness and peace by any easy method. There is certainly no holiness without tears for any of us.

Naturally speaking, she stood at the confluence of two racial strands: the Lombard and the Frank. The Lombards were warriors, vigorous, strong and energetic, and this she inherited through her father, Favarone. The Franks, her inheritance through her mother, Ortolana, were usually slighter in stature and less robust, a courteous, cultured and religious people, poetic and sensitive. The natural dynamic of Clare's development was that of any woman, to integrate the *animus*, the masculine qualities of her personality, which were partly composed of her Lombard inheritance from her father. Maturity for her meant finding peace between that forceful inheritance and the sensitivity of feeling which had come from Ortolana. With such choppy crosscurrents, she must have known considerable inner conflict, and the integration she attained is the measure of her psychic strength. All her life she reveals the Lombard energy, contained in the early years by her cultured upbringing. In the later Clare, we see the gentle Frankish side of her character to the fore, but energised and supported by all the Lombard drive and vitality. This is obviously an oversimplification, but it offers a framework for considering the inner forces that helped to shape her.

In the story of Agnes' flight, Clare is obviously stimulated by danger, far more than Agnes was. Circumstances would later oblige her to learn skills of negotiation, which must have been hard and distasteful, for her natural tendency was to carve a straight furrow of response. She comes across as highly intelligent, of great courage, physical and moral, deeply dyed with the inherited knightly code of fearless honour and defence of the weak, and all this she put at God's disposal. She had no hesitation in confronting the uncles to ask for custody of Agnes, retaining her self-possession even when they were violent and angry. She argued politely with the papacy and fearlessly tackled the Saracens without wavering or compromise. Her strong sense of self was like an inviolable tower, energising her under difficulties; she must have been a wonderful ally, a pillar of strength to Francis and the brothers and all who came to her. The down side of such great inner strength is that it can easily slip into autocracy or violence. In her heart she bore the weaknesses as well as the strengths of the code of honour and could easily have used all that psychic energy and power for her own ends; she must always have been a woman hard to say no to. She knew she was a natural protector of the weak. As a child she had kept back her own food to send to the poor [17:1] because, it seems, she felt a need to give from her substance not from her abundance, a need to share her very self with others.

Her sisters tell us that she exercised authority with great fear [1:10], but what had she to fear except her own bias to dominance? People who instinctively claim authority can find it hard to welcome the opinions of others, so her insistence on consultation and shared decision-making is particularly revealing. Even Francis, when they first met, was not accepted without question, although she 'did not withhold her consent for very long' says her biographer.[1] Her surrender came when she 'promised him obedience'.[2] It is psychologically consistent that she was cautious about accepting a position of authority for herself. She must have known that she could easily have run San Damiano on natural ability, but God was asking more of her than an exercise of patrician skills. She knew these were nothing to do with Gospel service. She obviously feared this natural ability in herself, and, so one witness says, Francis 'almost forced her' to accept the direction of the sisters [1:6]. Having once undertaken it, however, she then put her whole heart into learning to exercise authority as service, following the example she had seen in Christ.

Her words on authority show how deeply she pondered on her two great exemplars, Christ and Francis. Writing about the abbess, she draws heavily on Francis' description of the ideal superior given in Celano's *Second Life*[3] (although her omissions suggest that she hoped for greater maturity from her sisters than Francis from the brothers), and she also learnt much from Benedict. The paradigm of Christian authority, however, was found in St John's account of Christ washing the disciples' feet.

You call me Master and Lord, and rightly; so I am. If I, then, the

Lord and Master, have washed your feet, you should wash each other's feet. I have given you an example so that you may copy what I have done to you . . . Now that you know this, happiness will be yours if you behave accordingly. (John 13:13–17)

This was the origin of Clare's thinking about authority and the evidence shows that she lived what she taught, literally washing the sisters' feet, but in a way which made the sacramental dimension evident to all. When she set down the wisdom distilled from years of community living, she had the courage to say this:

The Abbess indeed, should have such [an air of] familiarity about her that the sisters can speak and act to her as ladies do to their servants. This is how it ought to be, that the abbess be the personal servant (*ancilla*) of all the sisters.[4]

In Clare's view, the abbess is responsible for the direction and government of the sisters, not for feudal power, lands, a standing army, rights of sanctuary, property and clout, as was often the case in contemporary great abbeys. She steadfastly refused property, and even the Pope was unable to move her, though it is indicative of her moral stature that he made such efforts to persuade her to adopt his policies, even offering her property and lands (not the normal practice) to support her impoverished community. When that failed, he suggested helplessly, and in vain, that he dispense her from her vow of poverty.

The positive gift of strong people like Clare, is that they not only have great vision but can also communicate it to others. This is reflected in the numbers who joined her, individuals as well as whole communities. From 1213 to 1238, sisters left San Damiano every year to go on foundations. We have a heartbroken letter from Agnes, sent to Florence as abbess, with no certainty that she would return. She and Clare had been through so much together that the decision to send her away must have been difficult, especially if this letter is a sample of the reaction:

I am burdened and tormented beyond measure and am almost incapable of speaking, because I have been physically separated from you and my other sisters with whom I had hoped to live and die in this world . . . I believed that our life and death would be one, just as our manner of life in heaven would be one, and that we who have one and the same flesh and blood would be buried in the same grave. But I see that I have been deceived. I have been restrained, I have been abandoned, I have been afflicted on every side . . . As a result distress utterly possesses me and I do not know what to do, what to say, since I do not expect to see you and my sisters again in this life.[5]

We might wonder how Clare felt when Agnes wrote about being deceived, abandoned and afflicted. Did she consider that her rather dependent younger sister would come to greater maturity out of her shadow? She was probably right, for in this same letter Agnes speaks about her new community with the voice of a competent leader, quite unlike the wild grief:

I have found great harmony and no factions here, which is almost beyond belief. Everyone has received me with great happiness and joy and has very devoutly promised me obedience and reverence. . . As far as the precepts are concerned, be assured that the Lord Pope has satisfied me, as I have said, and has satisfied you, too, in all things and in every way according to your intention and mine regarding our position on the ownership of property.

The 'satisfaction' the Pope managed to give was by granting Florence the same Privilege of Poverty that Clare had wrung from him. As far as we know, only four communities received this Privilege, which is interesting in view of its importance to Clare. It shows how far she was from telling others how they should live. She could easily, and reasonably, have insisted that if they wanted to use her name, they must live, or be allowed to live, by her form of life.

On a deeper level, anyone who resolved their inner conflicts as thoroughly as Clare, must have trodden paths of ruthless honesty. Because she became so holy, we must not fall into the trap of thinking that she had no inner darkness, no sin, no pain, no woundedness to deal with. Rather the contrary; she must have dealt with these more thoroughly, and we can well look to her for encouragement and guidance. She understood the shifts we make to contain our inner darkness because we secretly suspect the negative in us to be more powerful than the light. Had Clare not been into the darkness herself, she could never have become so light for us, never have left us such clear footprints in which we can tread as we tangle with our own dark inner destructiveness. Just as physical darkness is never definitively conquered, but always floods back at sunset, so we fear lest this be a paradigm for moral darkness, that that too will flood back when the light withdraws. It is interesting that Clare, caught up in this struggle, used to pray to the Lord of light in the dark chapel at night. Her reasons may have been quite pragmatic, but she was also acting out and externalising the nature of her interior struggles and conflicts, and doing so, often in great distress, before the crucifix which had spoken to Francis. In fact, distress was a notable aspect of her prayer in the early years. She wept a great deal and though this may also have been a consequence of excessive fasting (notorious for producing tears) it seems more likely that it was a discharge of tension, debris from the battleground within. There was also a cultural bias towards tears, not only for women, and to weep over the passion of Christ was not rare and was a gift highly prized.

Sometimes her powerful inner forces demanded expression, and appeared in her dreams as archetypal figures. Both Francis and Clare remembered their dreams, recognising them to be message-bearing, the unconscious mind telling the rational brain what was going on in the depths. Clare once had a vision of an angel – that is, a messenger – of darkness which stood beside her, formless in black, threatening her: you will become blind if you continue to weep for sin, it said cunningly.[6] Evil often gives physical expression to our spiritual dread, and Clare counters this, strongly affirming her trust: no one who sees God is blind. Words, at such a time, are not to be despised; saying them can strengthen us when we waver; the name of Jesus, like the thought of God, is very powerful in dark places, mysteriously routing the enemy on our behalf. This particular messenger of darkness vanished, but left a powerful memory. Since the apparition came in her sleep, the account, and perhaps the words, must have come from Clare herself. She calls the messenger a 'deceitful admonisher', in contrast to Francis who also admonished but in service of the truth. The messages of the deceitful admonisher are always false, challenges which we need not take up, for the lying messenger will always try to lure us into unnecessary conflicts so that we miss the necessary ones.

Clare's constantly reiterated conviction that she was a useless and unworthy servant, unfit to be abbess, grew out of these inner conflicts and profound self-knowledge. Such phrases were never just words or formulae to her, but felt realities,[7] and she laid it as a heavy responsibility on the sisters to replace her when she, or any other abbess, was no longer competent.[8] Her fear must have been that in spite of all her struggles, she would share her darkness with them and not the light of Christ. This adds another dimension to the insinuating threat, you will go blind: she feared to led them all into the ditch. Her biographer, speaking of her austerity and rigour, calls them a daily dying which she willingly endured in order to open her depths to grace, to focus her entire desire on the light.[9] Austerity and rigour were the means she employed to become less useless and unfitted, even perhaps means whereby to minimise the risk run by the others in following her. In her letters Clare speaks paradoxically of Satan as the true deceiver, using lies and guilt to wound us where we are most vulnerable, accusing us where we most fear failure.[10]

The conflict of light and dark is not only the fundamental myth of human striving (perhaps for animals and nature, too) but it is also the story of our redemption. The God of light entered our darkness and left footprints for us to follow. If we place our feet carefully in those prints, then in spite of our darkness, we will slowly learn to love tenderly, to act justly and to walk humbly with our God, as the prophet counsels us (Micah 6:8). Once we have accepted our weaknesses, then we will not need to deny those of others, and so compassion comes alive in us. Our hearts open up to the world's pain in tender and redeemed solidarity, and we in our turn begin to show others clear footprints in which to place their feet.

Over the years, God was working all these works in Clare. She was being formed into an icon of Christ our Ransom, the one who protects us from the powers of darkness and in time, she actually became what Christ was, a ransom for many (Mark 10:45). The year was 1240. Clare was ill and very weak. Rumours had come of the approaching Saracens, Frederick II's mercenaries, 'the worst of people', who had already attacked a number of convents in the Spoleto valley which, as Papal territory, was a particular target. The sisters' worst apprehensions were only too well founded. It was a Friday in September, about nine in the morning, when men broke through the enclosing hedge. Clare told the community not to fear because 'if the Lord is with us, the enemy cannot harm us', and then she said something very interesting indeed. She said: 'I want to be your ransom' [4:14]. She asked two sisters to help her up and to bring the Blessed Sacrament to her. This was kept in a silver pyx inside an ivory box, the custom of the time. Clare prostrated herself on the ground in prayer, begging the Lord to protect the sisters because she could not, and indeed, unless the Lord protected them there was no other rescue available. Gregory IX had been arguing for a long while that the community was too unprotected and here he was being proved right. Sisters Francesca and Illuminata, who were helping Clare, heard a voice saying: 'I will always defend you'.

Francis had said:

> for love of him, they must make themselves vulnerable to their enemies, both visible and invisible, because the Lord says: whoever loses his life for my sake, will save it in eternal life.[11]

Such a literal understanding of the Gospel always brings us up short, it makes us realise the extent to which our personal, self-protecting agenda stops us hearing what Christ really said. We might wonder how this teaching struck Clare at such a moment! Which were the visible enemies? Was fear a greater foe than Saracens? Francis also said that the perfection of obedience meant being 'subject and submissive . . . even to the beasts and wild animals',[12] and here were Saracen mercenaries, swarming like bees, says her biographer. It was an extraordinary invitation to live out this obedient vulnerability to mercenaries whom Filippa calls, with endearing impartiality, Tartars, Saracens and other enemies of God and the Church [3:18]. Such vulnerability, Francis hints, comes when we have made over our bodies to the Lord. In other words, it is connected with chastity, not so much in its physical aspects but in the generous choice of total self-giving, like Christ. Such vulnerability is, therefore, to do with integrity, with *honestas*. Clare herself had written to Prague a few years earlier that Agnes,

> in a terrible and unexpected way, [had] overthrown the shrewdness of the astute enemy, and the pride which destroys human nature, and the emptiness which infatuates the human heart.[13]

Now Clare had again come before enemies and again she found that her heart did not fail her. She had no sword for her defence, nor did she need one. How appropriate and significant

that Jesus spoke of himself as a ransom in the context of power
and dominance:

> You know that among the pagans their so-called rulers lord it over
> them and their great men make their authority felt. This is not to
> happen among you. No; anyone who wants to become great among
> you must be your servant, and anyone who wants to be first
> among you must be slave to all. For the Son of Man himself did
> not come to be served but to serve, and to give his life as a ransom
> for many. (Mark 10:42–45)

This incident with the Saracens was for Clare something of
what the Stigmata was for Francis, that moment when God
moved her life into another dimension. Having learnt to look
at Christ, she was now learning to see as Christ sees, sharing his
perspective. To be a ransom was the ultimate form of service.
She was caught up in the total servitude of Christ in his passion. She remembered his words to Pilate: 'You would have no
power over me if it had not been given you from above' (John
19:11); she remembered that one person is sometimes given as
a sacrifice for many. She remembered that the Lord had said:
'Take me and let these others go free' (John 18:9). This was
the focus of her long journey, begun all those years before when
she had left home to 'go to him outside the camp and share
his degradation' (Hebrews 13:14). Now that her hour had come,
she acted as she had seen Christ act. 'I am a hostage, a ransom,
for you.' Who could be more vulnerable to the enemy than one
sick woman before a marauding army? It seems to have been
Clare's gift to take Christ's words as literally as she took Francis',
while everyone else considered them impossible.

We must not forget that Clare was a woman who had been
bred and educated to understand the workings of power, and
this understanding remained, heightened, probably, by her
choice of powerlessness. The one who wrestles understands the
strengths and weaknesses of the enemy better than any. Nor
was she totally powerless, and she was now to summon up a
power which we have all experienced, namely the extraordinary
way that God can persuade us to choose freely what we do not
want! The Saracens were about to experience this for themselves. Tradition says that she stood in the doorway at the top
of a flight of steps and looked down on the troops. She said to
her community: 'Do not be afraid, they will not be able to hurt

us.' The dynamics of genuine non-violence are such that they generate enormous power which is not force but energy. No other energy is quite like it; it is completely without aggression and therefore without weakness. It is like light, like the glory on the face of Christ, penetrating all things yet itself totally penetrable. Such a light must have shone from Clare this morning, just as on a certain evening it had shone from the face of Christ. On both occasions, those who saw it were quite literally bowled over. The mercenaries, bent on rape and pillage, were suddenly overwhelmed by an alarm all the more effective for being unspecified. Some nameless, inner disquiet completely blanked out lust and blood-lust, ferocity, loot and every other overriding passion. Alarm crept through their hearts, swelling into panic until, Filippa tells us, they departed urgently, fiercely, as if driven away, anxious only to escape – from what? What was the nameless dread which stopped them in their tracks? What was the alarm which shouted down the most clamorous and irrational of all our passions? There must have been something about the way she looked, some translucence to God which halted them, some visible fruit of the long years spent mastering her own inner energies and letting light into her own darkest and most irrational corners. It was indeed morning in her life, the sun had arisen and shone upon her world, and both the community and the whole city of Assisi were saved from darkness that day.

What a guide she would be for us, if we could let her! She will teach us to confront our darkness and ally ourselves with Christ's confrontation of cosmic forces of destruction. When she had fled from home, it had been midnight. Now it was morning and the darkest hours of her life were over. All her journey now would be a progression, like the rising of Brother Sun, up to the blaze of noontide. The darkness had been a symbolic statement of the theme, the ground plan of her life. Just as she had travelled from solitude to community, from confrontation to brothers, so, as she experienced her inner darkness in solitary prayer at night, her community more and more experienced her as a clear brilliance in the Lord. This tension between dark and light which ran through her life brought her at last through a fierce spiritual crucifixion to a resolution which seems to us almost complete. As the sundial rune says, it is the shadow which reveals the light.

One Holy Week, Clare had become overwhelmed by Christ's sorrows, by his experience of the shadow. She remained absorbed until a sister reminded her that Francis had forbidden her to go for more than twenty-four hours without food, and Clare was amazed at the passage of time. We are conditioned to think that this happens easily to saints, but in fact it is not like that. The love that suffers-with is intensely painful, leading us into undreamt of realms of sharing. Our trouble is not usually our lack of love, because many people love God more than they realise, but our culture and our cowardice conspire together against pain. We fear and shun it, we evade it in a million ways, argue ourselves out of it, convince ourselves that, even spiritually, Panadol is better. Yet pain cannot be avoided; Christ's life and death are vibrant with its mystery. Once we have opened our hearts to Christ, his pain becomes ours. At one time, the whips which scourge us, scourged him; now the whips which scourged him, are scourging us. At such moments, all pain merges into the particular pain of Christ; his death lives in every memory, his feet are bathed in all our tears. The depth of the mystery is that 'he who suffered on the Cross was the Son of God as you are: tho' he seemed only a mortal man'.[14]

Once again there is this paradox, that all those years spent learning to love the crucified Christ made Clare into what we long to be: a happy woman. While her letters are remarkable for their spiritual quality and depth, they also glow with a simple happiness which catches at our hearts. When she first spoke with Francis, an 'insight into joy' opened to her.[15] She used to laugh, at herself and her weaknesses,[16] and in her letters she talks often about happiness. She uses the word *felicitas*, an everyday word used by the Romans as we might say: 'Good luck!' It has a pleasant, human feel to it. The root word, *felix*, is connected with *fecundus*, fecund, and, as so often, semantics contains insight. Man or woman, we are not happy if we feel sterile, with our creativity withered in any way.

When Clare wishes Agnes happiness, however, she also indicates that happiness is a choice, not a chance. She links it to our joy when we increase the talents the Lord entrusted to us (Matthew 25). The one talent, offered to all, is the joy of the Lord, and we must trade with it, reflecting it to others. This is partly why she says that the Lord has set us as a mirror.[17] In us, the joy of God is reflected, shining from one person to another like a series of angled mirrors in which our single flame becomes an infinity of fire. We must take care not to bury this talent in the ground of our native gloom instead, even if we do so in order to hand it back intact, for it will surely die if we do. Joy and happiness are for giving, for community, for fun. In the accounts of those who lived with Clare, we find a quiet woman of unquenchable delight, whose option for joy never left her.

Looking back to the passion of the scenes at Sant' Angelo and San Paolo, we begin to glimpse the extent of her journey. Once she had ceased to travel exteriorly and cast her anchor at San Damiano, she began to travel vast distances within. She came swiftly to such a reversal of materialist values that

> . . . the blessed father [Francis] realised we were not afraid of any poverty, work, trouble, the experience of being disregarded or held in contempt by the spirit of the age, but rather that we held this as great delight. . . [18]

No one, said a sister, could even talk about how holy she became unless the Holy Spirit helped them to speak [2:19). It was more than anyone had imagined possible, yet amazingly ordinary, as if she were a revelation of how we are all meant to be, given us to restore our self-confidence. If she said she is to be a pattern for us, then she must believe that we too can become full of light, clear and with no darkness of sin [3:32], that we, too, can stand before others as she stood, with an unveiled face reflecting the brightness of the Lord. Those who knew her, actually saw her grow more and more radiant as she was turned into the image she reflected, that is, the glory on the face of Christ (2 Corinthians 3:18; 4:6).

— 8 —

A Noble Example

❖

I am delighted when I hear reports about
the great integrity of your life.*

One of the gifts Clare brought to her task as a spiritual leader
was her attitude of encouragement to people. She writes, for
instance, to young Agnes of Bohemia in words which would
cheer anyone up, saying:

> I am delighted when I hear reports of your holy conduct and the
> great integrity of your life. This is common knowledge, and not
> only known by me but by almost all the world. As a result, it is
> not only I personally who rejoice but all those who do, or wish to
> do, a service to Jesus Christ.[1]

It is one of the hallmarks of greatness to enable others to do
better than their best, and Clare was no exception. Her skill in
leading others forward soon became known and she began to
exert a considerable influence. It seems that guidance in prayer
and godly living was as much in demand then as it is now, and
that serious spiritual endeavour was less and less the preserve
of a professional élite. Many people were responding to the
new ideas about the apostolate, to the changing situation of
the laity and to the consequences of lay education. God was no
longer mainly the concern of monks and nuns, and ordinary
folk everywhere were looking for the sort of guidance which
had, until recently, been largely reserved for religious.

Clare and her sisters, while remaining (unlike many similar
groups) in the mainstream of orthodoxy, rapidly became the
nucleus of a wider community of lay people who longed to
know God better. Single men and women came, young and old,
as well as married couples, who all committed themselves to a
regular life of prayer.[2] People were drawn by Clare personally;
they found her attractive and felt they could entrust themselves

---

*Clare, *Letter 1*, 3.

to her. They saw that she had some quality about her which they wanted to share, and many who, for one reason or another, were not able to join a community, did their best to live a 'regular life without a rule in their own home'.[3] With this kind of outreach in mind, the night watchman, Ioanni de Ventura, said that she begot many sons and daughters [20:7]. She taught them to live chastely, whatever their walk of life, to love poverty and to practise austerity, in what was then an appropriate manner but which now seems to us quite horrendous. She also encouraged them to open their hearts to God's great love for them and to learn the skills of love for themselves.

Clare's actual community at San Damiano was soon composed of women from all social layers, living in an equality which was completely new. They had established a situation in which there were no élite sub-groups and everything was shared. Some were well-educated, some could only sign their names, some could not read, but all shared in the work and the prayer, the laughter and the love as well as the hardship and the insecurity. It was the antithesis of the stratified, aggressive and acquisitive society from which they had all come. The originality of Clare's vision becomes clearer if we recall the mighty abbey of San Paolo with its powerful feudal abbess, its privileges, its standing army and great possessions, all continually being increased by nuns' dowries. The basis of the Poor Sisters' equality was their conviction that God had called them to be sisters to all the world. They were truly mendicant, that is, they looked to God to provide even ordinary necessities, so that they might be signs of encouragement to others, living examples of the care God has for the smallest sparrow.

As time went on, Clare's own spirituality grew deeper and her theological insights developed. Like the rest of us, she learnt as she went along, although her situation clearly forced her to articulate her insights right from the start. Sr Pacifica tells us that when Clare came from prayer, she 'admonished' and comforted her sisters, speaking the words which God had spoken to her [1:9], sharing with them what she had just learnt in prayer. For both the sisters and the brothers, the verb to admonish had become part of their language, but without the corrective overtones which it has today. Rather it meant a friendly reminder, almost an encouragement. Francis gave many such 'Admonitions' to his brothers, some of which are preserved for us. An *admonitio* has the flavour of encouragement, it indicates the oft-repeated, 'something she often said to us'. Following the same idea, a recurring symptom was also called an *admonitio* – a persistent reminder of mortality.

Gradually, Clare put together the fruit of her reflections in what we can now see to be a theology of reversed values. She said that the reason why God became

> despised, needy and poor, was so that those who were even poorer and more needy (starving to death in fact, for lack of heavenly nourishment) it was so that in him, such people might be enriched . . . [4]

Without God, we are only half alive, an empty shell. Our vast capacity, or our neediness as Clare calls it, and God's total generosity are meant to come together, so that all that is God's can be ours. The opposite is also meant to be true: all that is ours is God's. Together we and God build the house. Labouring alone, we labour in vain; working with God, co-workers and co-operators, we are caught up in a multi-dimensional design of universal wonder, which we occasionally glimpse but never fully grasp. Like the sisters at San Damiano, we are all permanent beginners, but also called to be encouraging examples to those even newer than ourselves, those just beginning to explore their destiny.

> The Lord has called us to this greatness: that those who are to be effective mirrors and examples for others, should see themselves mirrored in us . . . Therefore, if we have lived according to this form of life which I have already spoken about, we shall leave a noble example to others.[5]

Because she had found her Way, Christ himself, through the preaching of Francis, Clare was always very conscious of the influence we can have on each other, as well as our responsibility to support each other.

> And, to use the very words of the Apostle himself, I judge you a co-operator of God himself and one who holds up those members of his ineffable Body who are giving way.[6]

We should not gloss over her words that she is an example to us so that we can be one to others. She sees this as a small return for the love and grace showered on us by God. She appears to have drafted a spiritual knock-on effect from the

Source in God, to Christ, to Francis, to Clare, to us, to others . . .
What we must teach is what she will teach us, namely the art of
looking towards Christ, who is the original mirror; and Clare
urges Agnes to look into that mirror instead of involving herself
in bitterness and darkness.[7] Look into the mirror and learn how
to give a clear light in the house of the Lord.[8]

As such a light herself, she has much to teach us about
building community and the cost of it, about handling authority,
struggling with our inner darkness, grappling with major or
minor problems. Most of us live and work with others and for
most of us it is difficult. Like Clare herself, we usually find that
the components of our community are wildly incompatible,
designed, we might think, for maximum trouble. Yet community
is the house built by the Lord, and if the Lord build it, we do
not labour in vain. This holds true whether we are speaking
about a family, a religious community, a parish, a nation or the
community of nations. The existence of a group is as fragile
and as durable as the ordinary people who form it, each of
whom is dappled with good and bad, both monstrous and
heroic, all of whom depend on grace from God and forgiveness
from each other. Because of her stable form of life, Clare was
more of a community builder than Francis, although the
brothers might have avoided much pain had they allowed Clare
to teach them about listening to each other. In many ways, friars
and sisters represent something present in us all, and there is
something important to learn from each of them. Like the
sisters, we must all balance any parochialism in ourselves with
a more global and missionary perspective, and, like the
brothers, we must deepen and stabilise the vagabond in us by
touching our contemplative depths.

These are living issues to which Clare still speaks today. She
continues to draw us, sharing with us all she has learnt about
living in our endangered and lovely world. She tells us, for
instance, to leave land fallow, not to exhaust it, not to have
more than we need.[9] She would remind the others, when they
went out, to praise God for all the beauty in trees, flowers and
bushes, the creatures and people that they saw [14:9]. As a basic
attitude, this instantly removes us from exploitation of each
other or of our environment. She was deeply concerned about
the ordinary, the mundane and the practical and although she
found liberation from what her biographer calls a gnawing

concern for temporal things, she never despised them.[10] Her anxieties were often relatively small. She was troubled when they ran out of oil, concerned for the sisters' illnesses, for small boys who pushed pebbles into their noses, for the sick child of the man who coped with their finances [3:15]. This sprang partly from her natural human warmth and partly from the fact that she had been brought up to show just such a concern for those in her care. Above all, though, it found a solid theological basis in her fearless acceptance of daily life as a part of the wide creative love of God, her understanding that the small bread of everyday events is the bread which becomes Eucharist, thanksgiving, when shared with the Word made flesh.

There is also another theme running through Clare's life, which is that she lived intensely what we must all live to some extent. Just as a mirror concentrates the rays of light, so she gives a clear focus to what we practise in a more diffuse manner. Thus, she lived a life of deep prayer and withdrawal at San Damiano and is a symbol of that desert element which must be somewhere present in our Christian lives. She was committed to an absolute and radical poverty in imitation of the poverty of the Son of God, but we are all called to self-emptying in some degree. She lived in a particularly circumscribed type of community where problems of relationship had to be solved because they could not be avoided, yet almost every person on this planet lives with at least one other person whose needs cannot be entirely ignored. She tried, consistently and successfully, to relate each element of her life to Christ, especially as she saw him in the crib and on the cross. These aspects of Christ's life haunted her, and opened her eyes to what a paradox we all are. Poor, vulnerable and wounded, yet we bear within us our transcendent God. This paradox is like the skeleton, the bare bones, of our daily reality and many of our troubles arise from our unwillingness to acknowledge it.

As she saw it, we have an enemy, who might be without or within, but who is subtle and cunning in either case. She spoke in her first letter to Agnes about wrestling, using it as an image of the way we wrestle with our enemy:

Somebody who is clothed cannot fight someone who is stripped, because the one who gives more purchase is more quickly thrown to the ground; nor can we know glory in this world and reign in it with Christ.[11]

Reigning with Christ in this world is done from within our poverty, vulnerability and woundedness. Clare seems to be saying that glory in this world, temporal glory, is a huge cover-up, a way of evading the twin realities of our vulnerability and the Kingdom. If we want wealth and glory here and now, that is our choice and she makes no condemnation of it, she never suggests that it is an inadmissable choice, merely a foolish one.

> A camel can go through the eye of a needle before a rich man can clamber up to heaven.[12]

At the same time, she sees that the Kingdom is also here and now, not vaguely in the future, so the tug towards temporal power and glory is something from which we are constantly having to shake free. She does not automatically equate this world with sin and the next with godliness. Rather, we can live in either with God or without. We have choices which will depend on our values, but she points out that the values of temporal glory are not the same as Christ's, which reinforces her commitment to poverty. We are oiled with poverty, she said, so as to avoid surrendering to the one who wrestles with us:

> This is why you have thrown aside your clothes, in other words your temporal riches, so as to avoid surrendering to the one who wrestles with you, so that you can enter heaven by the straight road and the narrow gate.[13]

If we are cluttered and hampered with clothes, coverings and protection, then the one who is slippery will have no trouble in escaping our clutches, while we ourselves will be an easy prey because of all our trappings. Clare saw herself as someone in conflict with all that dragged her down, and again those things may come from within or from without, while poverty ensured that she was stripped for action, not hampered by too many clothes and not giving purchase to the enemy. These clothes that she talks about are the sort of thing the Lady Poverty meant by Avarice, Providence and Procrastination, all our attempts to control our destiny and satisfy our desires. On the whole, we clutch these things rather than live at risk, yet it is a doomed attempt, because the very things we cling to tie us in knots when we try to escape them. So she gives us a few warning maxims:

While we are giving our affections to the transient we are losing the fruit of love.

A camel can go through the eye of a needle before a rich man can clamber up to heaven. This is why you have thrown aside your clothes, your temporal riches, so as to avoid surrendering to the one who wrestles with you, so that you can then enter heaven by the straight road and the narrow gate.

What a great and praiseworthy piece of commerce it is,
to leave the temporal for the eternal,
to be promised heaven in exchange for earth,
to receive a hundredfold for one,
to possess the blessed and eternal life.[14]

When she speaks about leaving the temporal, she does not only mean the sort of radical and total option that Agnes was making. She would prefer to ask us one simple question: where are our affections? There will our treasure be. The choice is ours. There are the exchanges of temporal business transactions and there are the exchanges between heaven and earth. We cannot live without some involvement in the former but she sees no reason why our earthly transactions should not be executed in the spirit of the major exchange, the great and praiseworthy piece of commerce. Again, we have choices; Clare would prefer us to make responsible choices rather than to drift along going nowhere in particular.

An important and early step in making our choice is often the one of asking forgiveness, or of giving it. Clare maintained that our problems of relationships must be solved; we may not settle for silence. Relationships are like apples; one bad one will not improve the rest. If problems are left, ignored or unresolved, their poison spreads and will finally destroy everything.

... before she offers the gift of her prayers to the Lord (Matthew 5:23), let the one who gave the cause for disturbance, not only humbly prostrate herself at the feet of the other, seeking forgiveness, but let her also ask, quite simply, that the other intercede for her to the Lord that he forgive her. That other sister should remember that word of the Lord: unless you forgive from your heart, neither will your Father in heaven forgive you (Matthew 6:15; 18:35). So let her freely forgive her sister every injury she has received.[15]

It is our glory and our problem that we are responsible. Let the one who gave the cause for disturbance be the first to speak, instead of spending the rest of the day convincing herself that it was really the other's fault. Let her seek forgiveness, which implies accepting responsibility for what happened. Let her humble herself rather than blame and condemn, or start the whole thing up again. We see here the energy of spiritual realities, the way they never stand still. Either we continue to reach forwards to God, apologising and allowing our relationships to be repaired, or we join the problems of the world, compounding them with our own particular flavour. Though possibly not easier, it is certainly simpler to apologise to one person than to leave wounds to fester for generations. We have seen so much of that in this century, yet we still go on letting our small hostilities flourish because we find it so painful to lose ground, still more painful to lose face. Clare's response would be that such a loss of face is utterly irrelevant, especially when measured against Christ's example. He exchanged everything for nothing: the Lord of the heavens and the earth rested in a manger[16] – in temporal or worldly terms, the ultimate in loss of face.

This act of Christ's was, as Clare understood it, true poverty, far more profound than simply redressing imbalances. It opens up the vista of God's loving generosity in a way which moves our own living into a wholly new dimension. When we walk in Christ's footprints, she says, poor and of no account as he was, then we carry him within us spiritually just as truly as Mary carried him physically. It is as simple and as world-shaking as that.

> As the glorious Virgin of virgins did so materially, so you too, following in his footsteps, particularly the prints of humility and poverty, will undoubtedly be able always to carry him spiritually in your body.[17]

> Therefore be strengthened, for you are the beloved, the mother and the sister of my Lord Jesus Christ.

> And you have quite rightly deserved to be named the sister, the beloved and the mother of the Son of the Most High Father and of the glorious Virgin.[18]

Very early on, Francis had given her a promise, which she set for ever into her Rule and used to call her Form of Life. There are no instructions in this Form of Life, only a statement of an insight so fundamental and all-embracing that it would either

change her whole life or mean nothing to her. Even the words
sound honed and smooth with use.

> . . . through Divine inspiration you have made yourselves daughters
> and servants of the Most High, the King, the Heavenly Father, and
> you have betrothed yourselves to the Holy Spirit by choosing to live
> according to the perfection of the holy Gospel . . . [19]

This was the consequence of saying Yes to the Spirit, a Yes we
are all invited to say. Another example is Mary, the perfect
Christian, who also said Yes to the Spirit with her whole being.
She is our model and we follow her by doing what she did,
saying this Yes to the Spirit. It is a Yes which will never be without
consequences. What Francis means by being betrothed to the
Spirit is that a betrothal is a mutual commitment, a dedication
to a far-reaching creativity together. For us, it is a summons to
the heart of the Godhead and an invitation into the secret wine-
cellar. If we say this Yes, then what happened physically in Mary
will happen spiritually in us: the Son of God will take flesh in
our lives. We blanch at the implications of such logical and
simple thinking – and quite rightly, for they are life-changing
implications. Yet this, Francis and Clare maintained, is the
Christian destiny of us all. This is what Christ meant when he
said that those who did God's will were his mothers and brothers
and sisters. We are to bear Christ spiritually as truly as Mary
bore him physically.

It seemed obvious to Francis and Clare that God invites us to
share in this exchange by giving as well as by receiving. It
seemed equally obvious that we extend this generosity to the
rest of creation as well as to God, and that if we did share in
this way, we would all have enough. Francis used to say that if
he met a man poorer than himself, then he knew he had
stolen from that man. Applied globally, this would have radical
consequences on many levels. Christ raises the same questions
for us today as he raised for Clare: who is really rich and who
is really poor? She was always fascinated by this interplay of the
material and the spiritual. Mary bore Christ physically, we bear
him spiritually. Some are spiritually sick with affluence and
some starve physically. The desperate material need of half the
world manifests the desperate spiritual need of the other half.
Only Christ rescues us from the impoverishment of greed and
enriches us with the Kingdom of generosity. This is really a

further variation on the mirror theme, two kinds of poverty gazing at each other, neither able to heal itself, each in desperate need, 'starving to death in fact', and only Christ can enable us to make sense of it all.

It is one of the fascinating aspects of Clare's life at San Damiano, that she confronted so many of the tensions and dilemmas which still bedevil us today. We have seen that in the matter of money she had a different approach from Francis and saw no problem in it – or at least no new problem. While we do not know her mind for certain, we can make a guess. She was so conscious of God's holy working in the world through the Word made flesh that she had no fear of the future. She never saw growth and development as disasters but only as new areas of co-operation with God. Money, 'that tainted thing', can symbolise what we become if we surrender to avarice, or it can symbolise responsible stewardship. Perhaps the power of money lies in this, that more than most things, it reveals where we stand. Clare and Francis' time saw the opening of the story of money in the modern sense: it was a time when the great modern bankers of Europe were just about to start up in business. We, at the far end of that parabola, see the situation changing yet again. Money, as coins in the pocket, is vanishing. Computerised accounting is taking the whole system off into unimagined realms of abstraction. Clare can teach us not to be modern Luddites but to go forward with the assurance that God is still at work in our technological world, still creating it from within, still giving it possibilities and a future. As always, we are invited to bring the Gospel into that world, sharing our best with it as God shared the Word with us. We have a task of discernment and Clare teaches us how to do it. Guided by her, we learn to discern the Spirit of the Lord and his holy manner of working, and against this work, we assess our own.

An important part of that social discernment, she says, is to listen to the minority voice. We must learn to have difference without divisions, and to listen to the view of the minority. Often the Lord reveals what is best to the one who is the least, says Clare, slightly changing St Benedict's words. He says that the Lord often reveals what is best to the youngest.[20] It had always been a fundamental Franciscan conviction that the Spirit speaks to the group when they are all together, listening to the Spirit and each other. The ideal is always consensus, the Abbess is bound to seek the consent of all the sisters,[21] but Clare was a great realist and knew, as St Bonaventure was to say years later, that the more heads there are, the less likely it is they will think alike! The abbess' role, like that of any leader, is to inform, listen, consult, discuss and then, in effect, to say: it seems to me that the Spirit is saying this to us.

She was thoroughly convinced that the Gospel has been given us to help us live. Walking the way of the Gospel, we learn to sense the Spirit who makes our lives fruitful and creative, and this inner sense of the Spirit is a most sure guide for our journey. She asks us that, more than anything else, we long to have the Spirit of the Lord and his holy manner of working, and pray to the Spirit always,[22] for the Spirit is at work in us and we at work in God's world, and this is one and the same work. There is still chaos, worlds are still in becoming, but the Spirit still broods like a great bird over the future, so that the world may be created in the fullness of beauty. This is our way, let us walk along it.

— PART 3 —

Communion

❖

Communion means oneness of being. It is not that we ever become God nor do we become those whom we love, but we can and do become one with them in some essential way which is more than just having ideas and feelings in common. St John, in what must be the most pastorally reassuring passage in the whole of Scripture, tells us that everyone who loves, knows God, since love comes from God (1 John 4:7). Certainly that which we see between Clare and Francis is love speaking loudly about the presence of God. The more we reflect on their relationship, the clearer it becomes that it sprang from God, God was the source of all that they shared with each other. We would be much mistaken if we saw it as a medieval Romeo and Juliet affair which has endured because they made it respectable by spiritualising it. It is far more likely that by nature Francis and Clare had very little in common and found their commitment to each other arising out of their commitment to God.

Communion with God, then, is the basis of all other communions. Yet our communion with God often seems to be about the most intangible element in our whole lives. Without some kind of union with God we should not exist. After that very basic drawing of life, comes the union resulting from our efforts to co-operate with Christ, to share the Spirit's holy manner of working. Beyond that again are the upper reaches, more evidently a gift, less common and, dare I say it, less necessary. Such moments of felt awareness, or even of mystical union, may or may not come, but do, apparently, come to more people than one might have thought. Yet anyone who has been granted such moments knows that they are only the surfacing of something far more lasting, far more widely existing. They are the momentary appearance of a vast, subliminal reality, a transient

revelation of the enduring. The mystics, who live with such
awareness, are given to us as a reassurance; they breathe, eat
and sleep as we do, making little of it. They are overwhelmed
by an awareness of that union in which we also share, but
subliminally, making little of it.

In time we shall be led to the paradoxes in which all mystics
live, that God is in us and we in God, that we were always one
and are continually being drawn into further oneness, yet we
are not God nor is God us. We share our lives, yet our lives are
separate. God lives our life with us, and invites us to share the
life within the Trinity, yet we and God are never the same. So
union leads us into the painful heart of separateness which in
turn shapes us for further union, so that we are being continually drawn into the Beyond of God. The skills of this communion
teach us painful regret for our unprepared condition; we begin
truly to repent for everything in us which is not ready to go
further, which is unwilling to be bothered or too selfish to
endure the strain, too set to change. So our contrition continues
for ever, as our ever-changing standpoint reveals further areas
in us which are not godly and which must change, rather as a
new height climbed will reveal new valleys in the panorama
below. That process of climbing, of observing valleys and climbing higher still for a better view, is the process of conversion.

Clare and Francis

❖

What thou lovest well, remains, the rest is dross.
What thou lovest well shall not be reft from thee,
What thou lovest well is thy true heritage.*

When we think about Clare's relationship with Francis, either
to learn from it or to find encouragement in our own struggles
and delights, we can helpfully consider it in three broad phases.
The first phase is the time they had together, the second the
time of her grieving and the third lasted for the rest of her life.
In the first, Francis and Clare were establishing their form of
life, learning, praying and, apart and together, maturing in the
love of God and each other. During the second phase, she had
to come to terms with his death, to grieve and learn how to
carry, almost alone, the causes which he had held so dear. In
the final phase, all she had learnt from Francis had, after this
period of grief, to be interiorised and made her own. For many,
she became the embodiment of all that the Little Poor Man
had taught them. It was she who took on the role of arbiter
and guardian of the vision and it was she who kept faith with
Francis right to the end.

Deep in our hearts, we sense that Clare and Francis attained
something for which we all long, though we do not always
realise that the deep taproot of their love was their shared call
from God. It was not a transcended romance, though we often
see it as such. The romanticism, in fact, is ours and fairly inaccurate; the bond between them was not based on natural attraction
or affinity, but on a shared commitment, a shared sharing in
God, far more precious than natural affinity. In an essential
and, almost, in an existential sense they had a shared life. They
exemplified in their relationship what they most deeply believed
in, namely the Incarnation of Christ, as if, singly and together,
they each personified God's union with humanity. When we
look at them now, we see them glowing with the fire of love,
God's love for them, theirs for God and their love for each

*Ezra Pound, *Canto LXXXI.*

other, and it all seems to us one burning furnace in which they
are as united as it is possible for two people to be. They are like
the three young men, themselves tossed into a furnace, walking
about in the heat of it, glowing red-hot and yet not destroyed,
and the presence of God walking with them. It was not a godly
substitute for marriage, but something altogether beyond marriage, something nearer to that union of Christ and humanity,
of which marriage is an analogue. Surrendered to the Gospel,
they lived and related in this life as we shall all do in the
Kingdom which is to come. This was the real wonder of it.

Permeating their love was their shared vocation which flour-
ished once it was firmly planted in the soil of God. When Clare
speaks of herself as a little plant of Francis[1] she is not saying
something which we might find rather twee but possibly justified
by love; on the contrary, she is making a statement about the
gestalt, the setting, of their lives. They lived in God as plants in
soil, drawing nourishment from the humanity, the *humus*, of
Christ, and giving back the service of their fruits. By claiming
this title of little plant, Clare is saying that Francis had planted
her in the best soil going, for God is our natural habitat, the
finest soil for all our lives and all our loves. The story began
even before their first recorded contact:

> The Lady Clare, while she was still in the world, gave the witness
> [Lady Bona di Guelfuccio, a relative and neighbour] a certain
> amount of money as a votive offering and directed her to carry it
> to those who were working on Saint Mary of the Portiuncola, so
> that they would sustain the flesh. [17:7]

Those working on St Mary of the Porziuncola were Francis and
his first companions, in response to Francis' apparent misunder-
standing of the words spoken by the crucifix in San Damiano:
'Rebuild my church'. What had Clare heard that made her want
to contribute? Or was it one of those spontaneous actions which
begin a series of life-changing events? With hindsight we often
say, 'if I had not . . .' or 'if you had not . . .'. or, more painfully,
'if only . . .' Before he repaired the Porziuncola chapel, however,
Francis had also repaired the little church of San Damiano.
While he had been repairing the walls there, Francis had ven-
tured on a prophecy. Clare tells us that he

> climbed onto the wall of the said church and said out loud in the
> French language to some poor people who were living in the area:

'Come and help me in working on the monastery of San Damiano,
because there will be ladies here, whose famous life and conduct
will glorify our Heavenly Father in the whole of his holy Church.[2]

Francis loved the French language and tended to lapse into it
in moments of delight. His mother was probably French and
he may well have been almost bilingual. It was also, of course,
the language of the cultured classes to which the Bernadone
family aspired; Henry III of England, for instance, always spoke
French and knew no English, and Clare would have been able
to hold her own in it, too. This intensified the class distinctions
of the time, giving the aristocracy of Europe a common language as well as their network of marriage relationships. Clare
records Francis' use of it because everyone who knew the man
he became, would also know that it indicated his prophetic joy
in this little church, a church which was to symbolise something
that never failed him: the dynamic and visionary co-operation
of Clare.

Francis contributed the actual physical rebuilding and also
the vision of what was to come, it was he who saw the glory of
God which was to emanate from that place. Clare fleshed out
the vision. Clare was the light, San Damiano the lamp stand
which Francis made for her. It was Clare whose life glorified
God throughout the Church, Clare who was 'the firmest and
most precious stone in the whole building'.[3] Clare became a
rock for all those who longed to serve God by imitating Christ
in his self-emptying, a rock on which even Popes battered in
vain. No wonder San Damiano became, and still is, such a holy
place for the Franciscan movement. Yet, even today, it is not
just a place of memories, it is more like the mustard seed
of the Gospel, a symbol of small beginnings and God-given
fruitfulness. It contains, like all seeds, the genetic patterning of
generations yet to come, the people of their future.

We, projecting our own fears, sometimes think God must be
suspicious of human love, forgetting how hard it is to maintain
love without God, ignoring the question of whether there can
be any love in which God is not implicated. What we interpret as
Francis' and Clare's courage in relationship, is really a statement
about their belief in the love of God. Certainly, without the
vibrant presence of the Spirit, they would never have held their
love in balance. Precisely because love is so Godlike, it is never

easy for us to go beyond it. The leap to transcendence can seem like a denial of love, yet it was love, more than anything else, that the Lord had in mind when he spoke about the grain of wheat which needs to die if it is to bear fruit. This instinct we have that love should last for ever, should live happily ever after, is quite accurate and from God. Our mistake is often to glorify being 'in love', loading it with more desires than it can carry. We seek the easy, happy ending, the superficial resolution of conflict, and we fail to realise that we are settling for less love, not more. Our romanticism about Clare and Francis is short-sighted; they, with longer vision, looked beyond their personal world to a restoration for everyone in that Paradise where we shall again walk with God under a gentle sun, in harmony with all creation.

As they each listened to God's call, they approached the Kingdom of God like people entering their homeland, their complementarity beginning to show very early on. Through her confrontation with inner darkness, Clare was to grow steadily towards an almost unequalled experience of light. Hers was a spirituality of glory in which Paradise seemed already to have been restored. She was a living demonstration of Paul's words (2 Corinthians 3:16–18) that we, with our unveiled faces reflect, like mirrors, the brightness of the Lord, and so we grow brighter and brighter (in Latin *transformamur a claritate in claritatem*) as we are turned into the image we reflect. This was a key passage for Clare: given her name, how could she not feel that such words were written for her? Francis, on the other hand, had to leave behind his *jeunesse dorée* and learn, through alienation from his father, to take his first painful steps in identifying with Christ, who took upon himself our alienation from our Source. Francis' call seems to have been to travel further and further into darkness, and in the end to a total identification with Christ in his hour of greatest cosmic darkness. This was an unmapped journey of exploration into love and union, in which Clare was one of his most important teachers of tenderness. His earliest companions say that it was through the tenderness of his compassion that he was transformed into this living crucifix.[4] It is significant that after he had received the Stigmata, he came to San Damiano and Clare. There he had his darkest and most difficult hour, and was able to travel across that last hard tract of land because of her presence, full of light for him. It was as if, together, they girded the world, the cosmic conflict of light and darkness finally resolved in their two persons.

It was no easy victory. They both had a hard apprenticeship in gospel service. Just as Francis in San Verecundio, so Clare had become a servant in San Paolo. Francis, moving further into sharing Christ's passion, became another despised and rejected man, familiar with suffering and thought to be of no account (cf. Isaiah 53:3). Clare, confronting opposition, found her vision clarified and simplified, but still had to ratify that victory in every corner of her own personality and potential. In her compassion, Clare also travelled every inch of Francis' dark path, as she was to travel every inch of Christ's, and the radiance which was already about her must often have been to Francis a light, shining brightest in darkest places, a foretaste of the resurrection. Yet, as we reflect on this, we must not make the mistake of identifying darkness with pain, thinking that because she journeyed into clarity and he into darkness, therefore she journeyed out of pain and he into it. Both light and dark are revelations of God, if we have eyes to see. God was at work in each of them, singly and together.

When she 'cast the anchor of her soul'[5] at San Damiano, the threads came together more overtly. At Francis' suggestion, she began the Order and, when he 'almost forced her' [1:6], she became abbess. This was only one of the conflicts which speckled their early relationship. On at least three occasions, Francis had such a determined confrontation with her that the community remembered it forty years later. Neither was yet perfected; Clare's endurance could become either compassion or stubbornness; Francis' depth of feeling could be either creatively sensitive or deeply depressive. He could also be very autocratic, and just as he had to learn obedience, so he had to learn to exercise authority. Yet on a deeper level, when the sisters tell us about these differences, perhaps they are also saying that Clare was an equal of Francis. She was a free woman with a keen sense of her own vocation. By insisting she become abbess and accept Constitutions which would bring her life in line with the other groups of religious women whom Hugolino was trying to organise, it looks as if Francis did not, at first, fully grasp the courage and originality of Clare's vision of total poverty, lived in community. The sources make it clear that she would not have become abbess had Francis not insisted. They tell us nothing of the process by which he wore her down. Was her experience on this occasion one of those which clarified her commitment to making decisions by common consent, listening to the Spirit speaking through the community? Yet, although there were times when the vision was thrashed out between them and only resolved by a process of mutual adjustment, and though she was well able to stand alone, he was still vital to her. She says that when he died, she felt as if all her strength had gone. After Christ, he was her only encouragement, she said.[6]

This is precious evidence, because neither tells us much about the feelings in their heart for the other. We can only mark moments when their shared inner life seems to surface briefly. We know that Clare was integral to the development of the Franciscan movement, essential to the vision and prophecy of San Damiano. It was not by chance that she made her vows in the little chapel of St Mary of the Angels, where God had shown Francis the kind of life he was to lead,[7] and where 'the Mother of mercies brought both Orders to birth in her dwelling place'.[8] At San Damiano, too, Clare was a pervasive influence. 'The news of such things went far and wide in the world.'[9] She also helped Francis with major personal decisions, like the discernment about whether he should be a hermit or a preacher. He once told her to be ready to go to another convent, and she had no difficulty with this, always ready to fold her tent and go as soon as he gave the word, a degree of detachment which caused the sisters considerable alarm.[10]

In addition, all those men who had welcomed Clare to St Mary of the Angels, became loved and lifelong friends, keeping in touch with her through all the storms. They often spoke to Francis on her behalf, because they (like Clare) thought he should visit her more often. He was always cautious about women, and also cautious of the effects caring women had on susceptible brothers living a hard and tiring life, and, although Clare was a different matter, he was anxious not to set a precedent. Yet the brothers seem to have had no hesitation about contacting Clare, nor she them, and she several times sent messages to Francis 'by a brother'. Three of them, Angelo, Leo and Juniper, were at her bedside when she died, sharing her last great journey with all the ease of long-standing friends. For years, she had been their still centre, the symbol of their highest aspirations, the keeper of their hearts, a source of encouragement. Wherever they went, they returned to their sister at San Damiano who loved and challenged them.

Francis came to the hut at San Damiano – and why go there unless to be near Clare? – as it turned out, almost any friary would have been more comfortable, because his hut was overrun with mice which jumped around on the table while he ate. Not surprisingly, he became overwhelmed with self-pity. He was in a physical and spiritual extremity of ecstatic anguish from the stigmata, in pain from dropsy and his eye disease, he was blind, experiencing a final but profound inner and outer darkness. Clare made him soft moccasins for his wounded feet and later had an evocative dream about taking him a bowl of hot water to wash with. While he was in the mouse-infested hut, his last purgation of the spirit ended, and he emerged, singing like a blackbird, as he had not sung since the early days of the 'Herald of the great King'. He wrote a song for the whole of creation, he wrote a song specially for Clare and her sisters, words and music. Creativity poured unchecked from his integrated heart. When the Bishop quarrelled with and excommunicated the Podestà, who then forbade anyone to trade with the Bishop, Francis wrote a song to reconcile them, knowing that the Podestà's distressed daughter was one of Clare's community. He sent a brother to sing the newest song to the combatants, with a verse specially added about forgiveness, so that the Bishop ('I have a hasty temper, you must forgive me') and the Podestà ('I will make whatever atonement you wish') were reconciled that day amid great rejoicing in Assisi. Everyone had been touched – in soul or pocket – by their conflict.

In the early days, Francis had written the sisters a short, but cherished, Form of Life, which Clare wrote into her Rule lest it be lost. In this, he acknowledged that the same divine inspiration had called the sisters and the brothers, adding:

> I wish and I promise for my own part and on behalf of my brothers always to have for you, as for them, the same most loving care and special concern.[11]

This was more than friendly, it was juridical, in a Franciscan way. It was an acknowledgement that they were all members of one spiritual family, brothers and sisters to each other, to every person and to every thing. Like Francis, Clare also led huge numbers of people to a life of deeper prayer and penitence.

There is even a soldier's will preserved in the archives of Assisi[12] in which, wanting to make amends for all his ill-gotten battle booty, he appointed 'the lady who presides over the monastery of San Damiano near Assisi' as one of his executors. News of Clare, like news of Francis, had spread far beyond the Spoleto valley. Then there were the two occasions, in 1240 and 1241, when her prayers preserved the city of Assisi from the Saracens, so that she is, to this day, one of Assisi's principal patrons. Francis, they say, belongs to everyone, but Clare belongs to Assisi – though this last may be changing.

As we reflect on their love and mutual courtesy, their shared vision and their respect for each other, we begin to see that, because they revealed God to one another, they were also a revelation of God to all others. Clare, in fact, saw this as her primary vocation – to reveal God, reflect God's light and glory. She and Francis grew together through the struggles of conversion; they shared lessons of contrition, repentance and penance. They became skilled in communion – with God, with each other, with all others. They became exemplars of the rich possibilities latent in celibacy which, to be fruitful, must have a focus beyond itself on which we can concentrate our energies. No one will be fruitfully celibate if their celibacy is rooted in a refusal of intimacy, a rejection of human needs or a denial of sexuality. Celibacy is one of the pearls of great price, and it demands a high degree of spiritual commitment to maintain its focus and attain transcendence. Once the focus or the transcendent dimension have been lost, or if they were never there, celibacy rapidly becomes intolerable. We come to feel that all our relationships have become shallow or even impossible. Love such as that between Francis and Clare, celibate and God-filled, meant that their earthenware vessels became translucent to a light of great beauty. This is what it is all about. Francis became an image of the Son of God, a living crucifix, and Clare revealed the light of glory on the face of Christ.

As they learnt to express this human and spiritual complementarity, they gave to those around them – and to us – a revelation of the whole Paschal mystery. They both shared in the passion and death of Christ, both showed forth the resurrection, not to themselves or even to each other, but to everyone. Separately, they teach us much; together, they show us the whole Christ, suffering and risen. They show us a way of relating which is formed for the eternal relating of the Kingdom, in which we shall love to the fullness of our capacity, for Christ will be all in all. They speak to secret depths in our present relationships, where God is building an eternal love, even in us. They learnt the language of the Kingdom and they confirm that we can learn it as well. Most of us only do this when forced to it through the hiatus of death, when we – left behind – discover that if the relationship is to continue in any way, then we must learn this language. It is our native tongue but we have forgotten it and must relearn it, vocabulary and grammar, and then, like any new language, awkwardly use it.

Even for them it was not easy, especially for them perhaps, again because they went further. When Francis was dying, Clare also became seriously ill.

> During the week in which blessed Francis died, Lady Clare feared that she might die before him, for they were both seriously ill at that time. She wept bitterly and would not be comforted, because she thought that she would be unable to see blessed Francis, her only Father in God, before her death, for he had been her comforter and teacher and had first established her in the grace of God.

Was it coincidence that they were both so ill? Nobody seems to have thought so, nor to have thought her extremity of distress inappropriate. In a rather endearing way, when the protagonists were more high-minded than the romantic Italian temperament thought proper, the brothers and sisters seem to have made themselves responsible for helping the relationship along. They had made a very accurate assessment of this friendship, recognising it as near the summit of human love, seeing it as a great gift from God to each of them and, through this wonderfully enhanced ability to love, a gift to us all.

> So she sent word of her fears by one of the friars and when he heard of it, the Saint was moved with compassion for her, for he loved her with an especial and paternal affection.

Once again, and almost for the last time, we find the brothers acting as willing messengers, mediating the other's love to one or the other.

> He was guided by the Holy Spirit to say to the friar whom she had sent: Go and tell the Lady Clare to put aside all sorrow and grief, for she cannot see me now. But promise her that before her death

both she and her sisters shall certainly see me, and be greatly comforted because of me.[13]

This was curiously fulfilled, for when he did die, and they brought his branded body for her to honour for the last time, she did feel greatly comforted as she looked at the wonder of those wounds, but she was also 'filled with grief and wept aloud'. In the lament put on her lips by Celano, Francis' biographer, she pours out inconsolable sorrow. The serene reticence of years is stripped away and we look into a pit of naked grief, revealing more about the humanity of their loving relationship than we would ever have guessed:

> Why, she cries, did you not send us rejoicing ahead of you to the place where you are going, us whom you leave here in sorrow? What do you bid us do, shut up in this prison, us whom you will never visit again as you used to? All our consolation departs with you and no solace like it remains to us buried to the world . . . O most bitter separation, O unfriendly leave-taking, O most dreadful death.
>
> And when he had been taken away, the door was closed to them which will hardly again be opened to so great a sorrow.[14]

Years later in her Testament, Clare mentions this dreadful time, this unfriendly leave-taking. She speaks of how fragile she felt and how all she could do was freely to accept the inevitable, and gradually recover from the sense of having been tossed, like flotsam, into a hostile current. She slowly began to recover some sense of autonomy. Choices returned to her. Life slid beyond survival. Eventually she could acknowledge what 'most dreadful death' had done to her, it had left her robbed, literally be-reaved, stolen from. She gives us a kind of anguished shorthand:

> Again and again we freely committed ourselves to our Lady most holy Poverty.[15]

This is the only time in her writings that Clare uses the phrase so often on Francis' lips: our Lady Poverty. It may be that using his words made himself seem nearer, but it could well have been even deeper and more significant than that. The allegory of Lady Poverty was written just after Francis' death, and the experience it relates is the loss of Paradise and a long bereavement. This Clare could resonate with. She too had lost Paradise and entered a long bereavement. She may even have been the prototype for the Lady Poverty in the allegory. The opening paragraph of the *Sacrum Commercium* offers the Lady as a solid foundation of all else. With Francis gone, Clare was in need of such a foundation, for Francis had been 'our pillar and our only comfort after God, and our chief support'.[16] Like the Lady Poverty of Adam in Paradise, Clare could say of Francis: it was in my thoughts that I would be with him forever, for he was created just, good and wise by the Most High.[17]

So Clare entered, willy-nilly, on the last phase of her relationship with Francis. Only with the passage of years would she discover what all who have loved and lost must pray to find, that we ourselves have been most intimately formed and moulded by that relationship. Francis could never wholly die while Clare lived. He had changed her life; no death could alter that. She had been begotten in the Gospel by his vision, had shared his struggle and his suffering, had comforted him with her own strength and had wondered at the stigmata. She had been so irrevocably changed by this process that nothing could rob her of these things. What he had given her was not a possession but her own self. In time, she would discover that his words had been true: she would be comforted because of him, just as she had been grief-stricken because of him. The brothers knew, even before she did, that she had made her own all that Francis stood for. This is why those who had loved him most, loved her most. It must have comforted her to realise that they found him when they were with her, just as seeing him canonised must have comforted (and entertained) a woman of such faith. It was like a promise of future meetings. He had said: you will see me again, and she waited twenty-seven years until she could keep that appointment.

10

The Restoration of Paradise

❖

O heart, we have searched from end to end;
I saw in thee naught save the Beloved.*

Throughout the last years of Francis' life, Clare watched with awe as he was led further and further into a mystical union with God that was not only beyond the ordinary but seemed to be breaking totally new ground. God was doing a new deed, showing the Son to the world in a new way. For those who knew and loved Francis, it was not easy to find the border between him and Christ. Christ's own love seem to fill him to overflowing, like a river in flood, and the wounds of the crucifixion stamped on his body stunned them. They saw him as a sign of the new creation, they saw Paradise being restored in Umbria before their eyes. They remembered Isaiah:

> I am doing a new deed,
> even now it comes to light; can you not see it?
> The people I have formed for myself
> will sing my praises. (Isaiah 43:19, 21)

They came to think that both their personal growth and the phenomenal expansion of the Order, were all part of this new deed of God's. Through you, said Lady Poverty to Francis, the ruins of the heavenly city will be repaired.[1] It became clearer to them then that the purpose of our Christian lives is not narrowly to escape the gnashings of hell, but gloriously to restore Paradise, and there the best of all our relationships will find a fitting context. The paradox is that Francis revealed this not by might or by power, but by his weakness and vulnerability, by the Spirit of the Lord and his holy manner of working (cf. Zechariah 4:6). After he had received the stigmata, even simple acts like washing his hands had become a major problem. He who had been the support of them all was now the neediest of

---

* Jalalud-din Rumi.

them all, quite unable to manage his life alone. He could no longer care for himself in the most ordinary ways, so wounded had he become, and he was obliged to entrust himself to their care and thoughtfulness. As they shared his experience by serving him in this way, Clare and the brothers were filled with awe at this clear image of the one who was pierced through for our faults, knowing that by Francis' wounds too, they were all healed (Isaiah 53:5).

It is moving and significant that when we think of Clare and Francis together, we quickly find ourselves reflecting on the new creation. When they are both present, they open Paradise to us, because their relationship itself belonged so completely to the Kingdom. Totally given to Christ, though in complementary ways, they figured what Christ had prefigured, humanity restored and redeemed. Because they gave their lives to Christ, he taught them to live as we all shall in the Kingdom, and before our eyes they seem to enter into the glory of it, though we are hard put to find suitable quotations to demonstrate this. Our certainty is based on an awareness; it is rooted in a kind of *sensus fidelium*; it is a feeling we have about Francis and Clare together, that they were far beyond the ordinary, that in their generous and understanding love they mirror love within the Trinity and show us how this can be made flesh in our lives as well as theirs. They suggest that their shared sharing in the life of God can come to even further fruition in us.

In the Canonisation Process, Sr Filippa tells us about a dream of Clare's which reveals and illustrates this in a way that no one else would quite dare to do. The fact that Clare not only dared but was able to share it with her close friends, reveals the extent to which they were privy to her intense interaction with Francis. The Middle Ages made little clear distinction between dreams and visions, and Filippa obviously felt herself, in some sort, the guardian of Clare's memory, but surely she remembered the dream so much more clearly than we usually remember other people's dreams because it articulated something which she felt to be important and true. It made a statement about the relationship between Francis and Clare which Filippa recognised as accurate even though it was saying something that eluded ordinary expression. She tells us:

Lady Clare related how once, in a vision, it seemed to her she brought a bowl of hot water to Saint Francis along with a towel for drying his hands. She was climbing a very high stairway, but was going very quickly, almost as though she were going on level ground. When she reached Saint Francis, the saint bared his breast and said to the Lady Clare: 'Come, take and drink.' After she had sucked from it, the saint admonished her to imbibe once again. After she did so what she had tasted was so sweet and delightful she in no way could describe it.

After she had imbibed, that nipple or opening of the breast from which the milk came remained between the lips of blessed Clare. After she took what remained in her mouth in her hands, it seemed to her it was gold so clear and bright that everything was seen in it as in a mirror. [3:29]

In reflecting on dreams, our own and still more those of others, we should not forget the insistence of men like Freud and Jung, that the ultimate authority of the dream can only be the dreamer. The text of the Canonisation Process in which this dream is related, was not found until 1920, but already the dream has been analysed and considered by a number of authors.[2] Reading it today, not as historians but as people seeking help in their prayer and spiritual lives, there are still aspects which we can unpack for our instruction and encouragement. It is certainly what Jung would call a 'great dream', one of those significant and detailed dreams which give us a symbolic representation of some important aspect of our lives, or which tell us how things are, like a bank-statement of our psychological and emotional account.

In the beginning of the dream, we find Clare going to Francis with hot water and a towel, ready to serve him. She may well have done this during his illness; certainly there is no hint in Filippa's account that it was unusual, neither is there any trace of a fantasy fulfilment for something which circumstances had denied. The scene gains added poignancy when we remember how difficult washing had become for Francis after the stigmata. We also see Clare acting as *famula*, the household or family servant, or even as *ancilla*, the personal attendant, of Francis. These were both words which she used of herself, both words which carried overtones of intimate service, even slavery, both words of total dedication. The slave had no personal life apart from her servitude. This is what Clare means when she talks about the 'servitude of Jesus Christ',[3] that intense and generous dedication to others in imitation of the Christ who emptied himself of everything, accepting the form of a *servus*. The highest privilege in life was to be like Christ, the slave.

Francis is standing at the top of a steep stairway, on spiritual high ground in relation to most of us, but this presented no problem to Clare who quickly climbed towards him. She was like someone moving on level ground, she had no difficulty in reaching his heights; as we have already said, she was the equal of great people, a true partner to Francis. It also suggests that spiritually, she was moving forward even before she met Francis. It was not Francis who started her on this climb, she was already in motion, and more than that, travelling swiftly and easily. Nor does she come empty-handed. She brings herself to Francis in the form of two profoundly feminine symbols: a bowl and water. She brings him her capacity, all that she is, her openness and her receptivity and her ability to contain life. This is the symbol of the bowl. By the water in the bowl, she offers him life and specifically, her life. Like water, she gives life, to others but also to him; she was a partner not a quiescent disciple. All that she is and has lies at his disposal, poured out in generous service. The dream is also saying that her chaste love, itself indicated by water, is made fruitful by Francis. The water she brings him is hot, already affected by the burning desires of Christ, it is no ordinary water that could be used in several ways, but hot water to be used for cleansing, because her life already has a specific purpose. Because it is water for washing, this also suggests that Clare saw herself as giving Francis the ability to start again, to wash off the dust of life and be cleansed and renewed, that is – forgiven. Perhaps she is reassuring him, as she must often have done in life; perhaps she is acknowledging that we all, even Francis, must repent and be forgiven, must start again with clean hands and a pure heart.

When she reached him, however, the dream took an unexpected turn. Instead of her washing his hands as anticipated, he spoke to her, and did so in the words of the Last Supper: 'Take and drink'; and he bared his breast for her so that she could suck. He offered her his essence, his juice, so to speak, 'sweetness beyond description'. What a manifestation of love! He shared himself with her, as surely as Ortolana had. Marco Bartoli, in his study of Clare, makes the interesting point that in the Middle Ages it was customary for children to be breastfed for anything up to two years, or even longer. As a result, most people had genuine memories of being held at the breast, rather than it being, as today, a primal but pre-conscious experience, and – he suggests – this is partly why people of the Middle Ages were so uninhibited about the whole matter. He cites St Bernard saying that milk from our Lady's breast splashed on him in prayer, hardly a twentieth-century description. Francis was doing much more than this though, for what remained in Clare's hands at the end seemed like clear, bright gold in which everything could be seen as in a mirror. And this too is what love does for us, leaving the essence of the other in our hands like clear, bright gold and we see everything reflected in the brightness of this shining. We should also note that what Francis taught Clare was, above all else, to choose poverty, and it was poverty which was the pure gold he gave her. So there is a teasing understated paradox here as well. Having nothing but Christ's most glorious self is to have the richest gift of all, pure gold, tried in the furnace, seven times refined.

This brings us to the second level of this dream, and that is the way in which Francis reflected Christ to Clare. At that period, veneration for the wounded humanity of Jesus was intense, particularly perhaps among women, though certainly not exclusively so. It was often only through their spirituality that medieval women could come to any sense of personal dignity, and they found healing in Christ from the wounds caused by the almost universal assumption of women's sexual irresponsibility. Women at that time were primarily defined by their biological status, as virgin, wife or mother, and the Gospel did for women of the Middle Ages what Christ himself had done for them in his lifetime: it gave them dignity, freedom and maturity. Clare was only one of those who responded with intense personal devotion and gratitude. In this climate, mystically to drink from the side of Christ was to share in his death, and to be nourished by the blood of his resurrected life. It was a union beyond the sexual and beyond even that of mother and child. It was no longer union but communion, with all the implications of divine life shared and human life utterly given. In a similar way, Francis now shared his life and death with Clare, she was nourished by his life's blood, on every level of her being. That is the underlying statement of this dream.

In his first Admonition, Francis says that when we see the

bread and wine of the Eucharist as the Body of Christ, we do so through the Spirit and the Godhead. Then he pushes this a bit further and says that it is the Spirit of the Lord, living in us, who receives the most holy Body and Blood of the Lord. Like calls to like, he is saying, and if we welcome the Lord in sacramental communion or in the daily communion of prayer, it is because the Spirit is already dwelling in our hearts. So too, in this dream of communion, Clare is able to climb so easily to Francis because she shares the same Spirit of the same Lord and his same holy way of working. Through the Spirit she is given the new wine of the Kingdom to drink, so sweet and so delightful that it cannot be described. She welcomes Francis in this sacramental communion because she already had his spirit dwelling in her heart. Like spoke to like when they met. Francis loved Clare as Christ had loved him, that is, with a complete sharing of his life and Spirit. The transcendent holiness of their relationship has never been expressed more accurately than in this extraordinary dream.

The eucharistic overtones give their union in Christ an existential reality. Paradise was already restored. By sharing what Francis offered her, drink coming from his heart, itself wounded like the side of Christ, Clare was sharing in Francis' own identification with Christ. As with all symbolism, it is possible either to understand it in a narrowly sexual way, or else to reach for the wider and richer meanings. So this drinking from his breast can be seen narrowly as a sublimated, or simply displaced, act of intercourse, or more widely (and, as I think, more accurately) as a communion with the essence of Francis at his most Christlike. It was so sweet and delightful that Clare said she could in no way describe it.

It was also a sharing in Francis the mother – a title he often gave himself with regard to his brothers, meaning that he, like Christ, nourished his brothers out of his very substance. Here he adopts a mother's attitude towards Clare, too, nourishing her from his substance. She says in her Rule, however, that the love and nurturing a mother gives are not the pinnacle but the beginning of the love and nurturing that we who love the Lord should give each other.

> If a mother love and nourish her physical daughter, how much more must we love and nourish a sister in the Spirit?[4]

It is that 'how much more' which haunts us. Yet this dream reveals that she, Clare, who was Francis' first sister in the Spirit, had already received that 'how much more' from him. She knows it to be a real possibility, not romantic idealism. Francis, at the moment of being a mother to her was, like Mary, forming Christ in her. He also spoke to her like Christ, across all the barriers of time and space, even across the barrier of death itself. If Christ and Mary were bringing her into closer union with Francis, how could she feel alone? How could she grieve when her unconscious was telling her such mysteries?

In medieval piety, Christ was often seen as a pelican who, reputedly, pierced her breast with her beak so that her young could be nourished on her life's blood. This is what Francis was doing, and had always done, for Clare. In this dream we see Francis feeding Clare like a pelican. It was a message on many levels. You are my daughter, he was saying, whom I nourish, Christlike, with my own self; you are my darling who knows my very essence; you are my companion with whom I share the secrets of my heart; you and I are one flesh and one blood because we are true sharers and partakers in the body and blood of Christ. It is almost as if she had become, for him, all the paradigms of women: at once virgin and wife, daughter and widow, disciple and teacher, pupil and wisdom herself; but she was much more than this as well.

We find even more dimensions to this dream if we explore, a little, their understanding of what it means to be a mother in Christ. In the Form of Life which he had written for Clare, very early on, Francis had said to her and her sisters that they had united themselves to the Holy Spirit. This idea grew out of his thought that like our Lady, Clare and her first sisters had made themselves handmaids of God by sharing the servitude, the *servitium* of Jesus Christ. They had imitated our Lady by saying Yes to God. When we do this, ran Francis' thought, we open ourselves to the Spirit of the Lord who overshadows us, and Christ is born again in our lives and in our world. For Clare and Francis, Mary was the perfect Christian, the model of all that we are called to be. What else did Mary do in her life but bring Christ to birth in the world? This they saw as our task, this is what our Christian lives are all about. This is why he used to call Clare Christiana, the Christian, Christ's Lady.

Francis called Mary the 'virgin made Church', meaning that

she literally became the place where Christ dwelt, his home, his robe, his servant and his mother.[5] She was the virgin made Church because she nurtured Christ by her loyalty and support all his life long, just as Clare had done for Francis. Mary was the virgin made Church because she teaches us the skills of discipleship, showing us how to think about ourselves in relation to God, the Trinity. She is an exemplar, like a sampler showing all the different stitches which link us to God. She is:

> the daughter and servant of the most high and supreme King and Father of heaven, mother of our most holy Lord Jesus Christ, bride of the Holy Spirit.[6]

She is also the Church because she advises us, as she did at Cana, to do whatever he tells us (John 2:5). Francis and Clare saw this decision to do whatever he tells us as the ground plan of discipleship, but, because doing what Christ tells us inevitably leads to sharing in Christ's life, death and resurrection, it is not simply a matter of reorganising our daily routine. It is more profound than that, a summons to surrender our hearts not to glory, but to fragility.

Mary was glorious because Christ received our human nature from her, and in such a way that he shared what Francis calls 'the flesh of our frailty'.[7] She gave the flesh of her flesh to form a vulnerable Christ, she taught him her own tenderness with which, in the flesh of our frailty, he became a pelican to us. In that same flesh of our frailty, Francis was a pelican to Clare, and she to others. This sort of leadership has nothing to do with roles and positions, but everything to do with communicating life. It is the truest act of love. By it we, like Mary, bring Christ into the world of our time. No wonder they loved the virgin made Church so sensitively, were so aware of her sorrow. Time after time, Clare put her forward as an example of how to live so that God is first in our lives, not because this is what the devout (if such we are) ought to be doing, but because it is our privilege as Christians. She saw how immense were the responsibilities given to that young girl. She bore such a Son, Clare says, as the heaven of heavens could not contain and she held him on her young girl's lap.[8]

This same high calling is ours today. If Mary is relevant for us, it must be because she has a deeper message than honouring physical virginity. In Mary the virgin, Francis and Clare saw that inner citadel of self which admits of no compromise, and which it is our glory to offer to God. Eckhart (1260–1327) speaks about the certain pinnacle of the soul, meaning that core of our being which only God can touch, where there are no other relationships or interactions, an Everest of the spirit where there are no footprints. This certain pinnacle of the soul is what Mary's virginity means for us, personally and for humanity. It is the still centre of ourselves from which we are too often alienated and we need to find our way back. Mary is a herald, a promise of that integrity which can be ours, a sign of how we shall be in Paradise when we too stand in the image and likeness of God.

Clare's letters are filled with her awareness of these hidden and almost mystical paradoxes of Christian living. She speaks of poverty bestowing riches, the Kingdom promised to the poor, the hundredfold in place of one. She speaks about losing in order to receive, loving in order to be chaste. The choice of poverty is an option for emptiness in order to enlarge the space of our hearts; and, in this perspective, she slowly found a path through Francis' death. She did not need to like it, only to survive it, to experience that an inner emptiness is sometimes part of the journey. In one profound sense, we always travel alone. For that inner solitary who dwells at the pinnacle of our being, the desert must take priority. There we struggle with our personal demons, and unless we do, our lives will always lack deep foundations so that our house will one day totter on its sandy base. In the desert – wherever it may be, within or without – we are realigned, rather as iron filings tossed on paper are realigned along lines of force by the command of magnetic power. We rest in the desert, like iron filings on the paper, until the magnetic power of God has done its work, making us fit for communion, but although the iron filings of our nature change their pattern, they retain their nature. We always remain unmistakably ourselves. This is why our petulant demands for love so often bring us only a deeper sense of isolation. We bring to communion what we are and nothing more, and our painful paradox is such that although we are formed for communion, we only come to it through solitude.

Because she gave her true self to love, we meet in Clare a clearly defined person who feels the same at each meeting. The mature Clare is in line with the young Clare. She was always deeply preoccupied with the magnetism of God, and said that the prime fruit of that force is love and the chastity which accompanies love. Purity comes when we place Christ at the heart of our lives; integrity and virginity come when we have fully accepted Christ and his Gospel, been thoroughly realigned by God.

> Loving him, you are chaste,
> touching him you are made pure,
> taking him to yourself, you are a virgin.[9]

The integration of her own sexuality expressed itself in everything she did. The fact that she could relate this dream at all, not only to Filippa, her lifelong friend and contemporary, but also to her niece and another younger woman, suggests that she was very confident of herself on the sexual and emotional levels. In an age every bit as preoccupied with sexuality as our own, her silence on it in her Rule is interesting, particularly when we compare it with, for example, the Rule of St Augustine which gives long and detailed instructions for keeping each other on the straight and narrow path. It suggests that Clare's interest lay elsewhere, with our power to love rather than with sexuality as an exploration of the body's responses. She seems never to have thought reductively, but always searched for the inwardness and the rich heart of any matter. This gave her what we often lack, a conceptual framework to give meaning to a sexual dynamic which none of us can ignore. This is important for us today because, on the whole, we are so mixed up about sexuality. It is shouted from every hoarding and ghetto blaster, and the consequent devaluing of such a force does us no good.

Perhaps one powerful reason why Francis and Clare are so relevant today is that, singly and together, they transcended this powerful force which defeats so many people, and yet they emerged at the end of it as radiant examples of the way we would all like to be. We sense, and rightly, that the relationship we hanker after is far in front of us down a long road. When we see the inner dimension of their love, as we see it in this dream, for instance, then even we, children of the Instant Age, can believe for a moment that when our love is sown in the good soil of God, it will indeed bear fruit a hundredfold. We may search from end to end, in the words of the poet, but until we find the Beloved, Christ, in the heart of our love, we are grasping smoke, burning our hands in the flame.

Christ our Way

❖

The Son of God has become the Way for us,
and our most blessed father Francis
showed and taught it to us by word and example.*

As Clare grew older, she increasingly found her strength in Christ weak, crucified, dying. Looking at him, and reflecting on her own experiences and those of others, she saw more and more that Christ is not only with us in our pain, but that all pain is somehow garnered up in him, honoured and kept for an eternal harvest. This conviction gained in depth when the wounded Francis came to San Damiano, so glorious and so holy, yet so weak and helpless, and therefore such a powerful and moving revelation of Christ. It was as if all she had learnt about the reversal of values had been moved onto a completely new plane of sharing and participation. The unbelievable reality of Francis led her into a spiritual dimension in which our pain is God's pain, in which Christ not only bore the sins of humanity but also the terrible wounds, the anguish, the dilemmas and even the depravity of being human. As a result, Clare learnt to make Christ the focus of all the situations, good, bad and indifferent, which abutted onto her own life. She also saw, looking at Christ on the cross, how he had entered into those very aspects of human life which we most avoid and deny. Through this *ineffabilem caritatem*, this love which cannot be explained, he had opened all our pain onto glory.[1]

Meanwhile, the crucifix which had begun everything by speaking to Francis hung at San Damiano. Before this strange and rather archetypal Christ, Clare prayed daily from the age of eighteen, ceaselessly honouring that luminous beginning, continually exploring the mysterious paradox of Christ crucified. When she speaks so powerfully about gazing on Christ, does she have this crucifix in her mind's eye? It is a curiously stylised figure with wounds like stars, radiant and radiating.

---

* *Testament of Clare*, 5.

Christ looks almost peaceful, gazing deep into some vision. Up above, the angels are smiling as they welcome the risen Christ back to heaven, mission accomplished. Round about, people stand in groups, stirring with wonder, like people after terrible trauma who slowly realise that all is well. The flame of his figure stands out from the others, from all the market-place people, living and moving in another dimension.

On this crucifix, Christ is both gloriously involved and deeply alone. He is on another scale from that of the bystanders, suggesting his greater being and longer perspective. He transcends the ordinary, yet he is unmistakably one of us; at the same time, he gazes into some infinite distance to which we are almost blind. Over his head is a faint, translucent veil, indicating that like Moses, he reveals the glory of God which we cannot bear unless it be veiled. In the bottom right-hand corner, St Peter's cock is there, crowing away, to remind us of our fragility. It is a crucifix filled with the sound of voices, potent with revelation and fulfilment. Christ stands rather than hangs, a pillar of fire leading us into the desert, which is both a beginner's place and an expert's, a place for spiritual children and for mature spirits. In the beginning of our conversion we are often drawn, as Francis was, to nature and wide open spaces, preferably empty of people. After our journey into the love of God, we may come again to nature and wide open spaces, but this time they will be flooded with the glory of God and the pain of the world. In the beginning, we need wide spaces to contain our sound and fury, but later, when our loneliness and alienation have opened onto the wider tundras of the spirit, we find the spaces resonant with God, each tree, bush and bird a revelation.

Particularly in the early years of her life, Clare moved in a spiritual climate of extraordinary fervour. The beginnings of the whole Franciscan movement were profoundly charismatic, and this crucifix stamped its message on their hearts, forming their spirituality. An incandescent love spread from the crucifix to Francis and Clare, and from them to the others so that they all glowed with the Spirit. Their feelings of love and their awareness of sinfulness were intense, moving easily into eloquent expression. There was a great depth of sharing among them all, a joyous retelling of their passionate experiences of Christ. There was no group conformism, very little planning, and they survived some amazing mistakes and rash decisions. It must be admitted that some of them were quite odd, but they all had such mutual respect and such appreciation of the strange works of God, that oddness was a kind of grace. They were living demonstrations that for those who love God, all things work together for good, even sin, as Augustine adds, and even eccentricity. Part of the reason why the stories about them are so delightful is because each one was living his or her own ardent relationship with Christ with immense energy and originality, with so great a love that everything else dwindled in comparison. Clare said to Brother Rainaldo towards the end of her life:

> My dearest brother, since I knew the grace of my Lord Jesus Christ through his servant Francis, no hardship has been a bother to me, no penance has been difficult, no weakness has been hard.[2]

Yet in spite of this, and in spite of the astounding expansion of the Order, these were no easy years, either for Clare and her community or for the brothers. It was probably in 1221 that the friars gathered in Assisi and were found to number five thousand, presenting Francis with an unexpected – and unwanted – organisational dilemma. The same year Peter Catani, to whom he had thankfully relinquished the government of the Order, died, the first of the early companions to go. Several of them were to live even longer than Clare, bringing home to us how young they all were at this time, most of them in their early twenties. These were also the years of expansion beyond the Alps, including some unplanned fiascos, like the group who went to Germany knowing only one German word: Ja, which they said to everything, thus landing themselves in some tricky situations. In 1224, they came to England. 'O misery,' said a Benedictine chronicler, 'O more than misery, O cruel scourge, the Friars Minor came to England'!

Somewhere between 1224 and 1227, Brother Juniper, whom Clare, like Francis, loved with a special tenderness, was picked up by the guards of a local war-lord[3] and tortured. A cord was tied round his head and tightened with a stick like a tourniquet, compressing his skull. He was then racked and, with his feet tied to the tail of a horse, dragged to execution, being rescued by another friar just in time. Juniper, never strong on rationality, was left severely weakened by this treatment, but his heart was so given to God that he filled Clare with joy whenever they met. Even standing around her deathbed, he poured out for her 'sparks from the furnace of his fervent heart'.[4] Because he had been through so much, he never complained about ordinary things, so (as is the case with uncomplaining people) he was often sent to live with particularly difficult friars! Soon after the torture, Brother Tendalbene, Brother Strive-for-Good, entered the Order and took Juniper under his wing. When Tendalbene died in 1255, the gentle, uncomplaining Juniper went berserk with a kind if elemental fury, smashing up all the household utensils of the friary, saying that now his brother had died, this is how the whole world was for him – in pieces, smashed and broken.

Clare may not have been going to smash up the household utensils of San Damiano, but when the brothers took Francis' dead body away and the door closed behind them, enclosing her with sorrow, was there any black pit into which she did not descend? In that terrible first year after Francis' death there was also such a famine that the people were eating nutshells and tree bark and there were rumours locally of cannibalism.[5] What was the inner symbolic anguish of that famine for Clare, struggling with the emotional and spiritual famine of Francis' absence, to say nothing of her anxiety for her sisters? What did famine mean for a community dependent on gifts for their food? Was it at this time that Sr Andrea contracted scrofula, which is tuberculosis of the lymph glands in the throat, a disease associated with overcrowding and undernourishment? It seems that Andrea, in her despair, had tried to kill herself [3:16][6] – a situation which Clare handled with intuitive sensitivity and some straight talking. Already Clare was finding something which eight hundred years of experience has only confirmed, that the enclosed contemplative life yields its joys in the measure of our surrender to it. Lived without that total commitment (as Sr Andrea appears to have been doing) it is a kind of hell, leading in the end to despair. Add all this to the twenty or more foundations and the correspondence and business involved, and add the conflicts among the friars, and we have a picture of very difficult years, to which Clare must have looked back as to a nightmare.

The thirties were also years when the vast and controversial Basilica was being built in Assisi, when the friars grappled with post-conciliar demands for greater scholarship, and Clare's friend Elias, the only Minister General besides Francis who was not a priest, headed for dismissal. He had gradually slipped into softer and softer living, keeping his own cook and riding, says Salimbene scornfully, on a plump palfrey. The Order which had begun in such joyous brotherhood, was being rent apart with arguments and bitterness. One General Chapter after another passed decrees which slowly brought about a two-tier system of clerics and non-ordained brothers, far from the dream of total equality in Christ. Clare made no judgements but no compromises. She struggled resolutely with Pope Gregory IX (1227–1241) about her determination to live in total poverty, and learnt peacefully to accept a *de facto* marginalisation and the apparent loss of Gregory's esteem. Many other things had also happened in those turbulent years, but these are enough to show that our image of perpetual joy in a never-ending springtime of the spirit is not based on external delights.

The facts speak for themselves and the struggle is reflected in Clare's spirituality. God is not (as we are) waiting for things to get better but is working like yeast in the most dough-like times of our lives. God comes where we already are. There is no need to change everything before we find God, and we can draw strength from remembering the way joy blossomed around Clare in spite of the difficulties she had to contend with. God requires nothing of us, said Angela of Foligno a few years after Clare's death, except that we love him. It seems such a modest requirement, yet we are so contrary that it is far from easy for us to allow love for God to dominate our lives. Clare gave herself so generously to this love that she was led into a fully restored humanity, characterised by balance and harmony. We see this in almost everything she says. It is also reflected clearly in her Rule which, finally approved at the end of her life, is a model of wisdom and realism. She was skilled in the checks and balances which assist our search for harmony and she knew the art of creating a way of life which was rounded and at rest within itself.

From this still centre, she and her sisters were able to share with others what had been given to them. When the brothers were torn apart by dissension, Clare dealt with this by opening herself to the love which inflames us to greater love. When conflict destroyed courtesy, she steeped herself in the graciousness of God. When Juniper was literally rent apart under torture, she could give him the overflowing gentleness of God. When Francis died, she learnt to seek him in the One whose fragrance is such as to bring all the dead to true life again.[7] At every turn, she sought the resources she needed in God. This was part and parcel of the way she realised (in every sense) the full implications of the Incarnation. It was also the way she learnt to live in the fullness of her own warm, loving, clear-sighted and dedicated human nature.

All this was no easier for Clare than it is for us. Besides grief, physical distress and the pain of compassion, she also knew the distress which follows when the dreams to which we have given our lives are rejected by those we thought had shared them. Yet in spite of this, she was always resourceful, always eager to co-operate with Christ, to share the Spirit's holy manner of working. When things failed to work out, she never seems to have panicked and given up, assuming (as we often do) that it must be her fault. Because she listened to God with no hidden agenda of her own, she had a remarkable ability to stand by her decisions. She learnt to entrust her fallibility to God as well as her good intentions, and having done this, she took her own advice and strengthened herself in God's service, continuing to go from good to better and from strength to strength.[8] She shows us that growing from good to better is, like happiness, a choice and not a chance. For Clare, Christ became the '*tu*', the 'thou', of her life, and in the exchanges of prayer she and Christ revealed their essential mystery to each other. When we also commit ourselves to Christ, we also will discover that he is, as he said, the doorway of God who is the true life, and only human lunacy would dream of living without life.

On the community level, this spirituality of exchange was lived out exteriorly as material poverty and almsgiving, The sisters lived entirely on what was given them but they also worked hard, spinning, weaving, making things with the cloth, the proceeds of which were for others, for giving away. So even materially their way of life expressed this spirituality of exchange, and was quite different from the monastic ethos of self-sufficiency. Clare was not acting out of idealism but logically developing her insights into the meaning of following Christ. She was not seeking simplicity of life-style for its own sake, nor to avoid being a burden to anyone, but only to do what she had seen Christ do, to live by sharing and generosity. It was risky, but that is part of the reality of being poor. It depended on others who were under no obligations or contract, but it was not a wild act of irresponsibility. It was a free choice of vulnerability over aggression, of littleness over power, of physical hardship over luxury. It was an option for those at the bottom of the pile, a decision to be among the exploited rather than to exploit. She learnt it from Christ, who was laid in an animal's crib, nailed on the cross as an example, a *speculum* for us:

> In this mirror is a shining reflection of blessed poverty, holy lowliness and love beyond words, as, by the grace of God, you can contemplate ... [9]

Clare's teaching was, and still is, so powerful because it is so possible. We sense the truth of her conviction that by accepting our innate poverty, we discover it to be full of the presence of Christ; that however difficult or dreadful our lives might be, Christ is in our lives living them with us. Often the absentee from our reality is not Christ but ourselves, busy as ever with denial. Nor is Christ present in a passive way. He is always at work. 'The Father has never yet stopped working and I am working too' (John 5:17). Because this work is still going on, we need to keep our eyes on the worker, Christ, especially in the culmination of his work as we see it on the cross. It is constantly coming to fruition in individual lives and even, in some mysterious way, through the tragedies of history. You will hear of wars and rumours of wars, said Christ, and with what truth, but the Kingdom is not yet. All we know here and now is in Christ. This is why Clare continually tells us to contemplate that love, gaze at him, consider him, to long to imitate him.[10]

> Contemplate the unimaginable love through which he was willing to suffer on the Tree of the cross and, on that same Tree, to die the most disgraceful kind of death.[11]

All this was not for nothing, nor was it done by chance. Christ on the cross is a message full of meaning, teaching us how to endure without bitterness,

> so that, like another Rachel, you may keep your objective in mind, always looking to the beginning. Hold fast to what you now hold, never cease doing what you are doing now.[12]

By 'the beginning' Clare means Christ. *Principium* is the Latin word she uses, she who read the Gospels in Latin and remembered Christ answering the question: 'Who are you?' with the words: *Principium, qui et loquor vobis* (John 8:25). Modern translations interpret it as: '(I am) what I have told you from the outset' (JB) which may be more probable in terms of scriptural scholarship, but 'the Beginning, who also speaks with you' is what Clare read when she pondered John's Gospel. If we keep our eyes on Christ, we will never lose sight of where we are going; this is what she is saying to us, not for the first time.

Like her, like every saint since Abraham, we too will find that the covenant is not our commitment to God but God's commitment to us. It seems as if this lesson is only learnt in darkness, through purgation by fire. As we undergo this purging, the quality of the darkness changes. It ceases to be a place of fear and trial, and becomes a place in which every light is clearly seen. It becomes a context for the light, the true light, from which any tiny stump of a candle can catch the flame, even we ourselves. This opens up a further slant on Clare's earlier identification of darkness with her inner sinfulness, or with that 'thing' which we all have and which represents our greatest dread, our greatest apprehension about ourselves. Because Christ entered so fully into our nature, then even – or particularly – our greatest dread will become the very chink through which God comes into our lives. Not only that, but our wounds will become the means by which others are healed. In the graciousness of God, this is a sharing in redemption. We are being made Christlike for others, made like the one by whose wounds we are all healed (Isaiah 53:5). God offers no magic answer to the pains and problems of life, but the merciful and generous alchemy of God does something more, it shares and transfigures our anguish from within, making it redemptive and creative for others.

We are so made in God's image and likeness that everything in us is capable of prefiguring and preparing us for the depths of God. Many of us live our lives in what might be called a 'pre-God condition' but this is not God's vision of things.

> Be conscious, said Francis, of the wondrous state in which the Lord God has placed you, for he created you and formed you to the

image of his beloved Son according to the body, and to his likeness according to the spirit.[13]

Gazing at the crucifix we see all this as in a mirror; we see the likeness in which we are formed and we see that likeness itself informed by our pain. We find that all the paradoxes we have touched on come to their focus in this, that Christ is most like us just where we are least like him.

> Ours were the sufferings he bore,
> ours the sorrows he carried.
> But we, we thought of him as someone punished,
> struck by God, and brought low.
> Yet he was pierced through for our faults,
> crushed for our sins.
> On him lies a punishment that brings us peace,
> and through his wounds we are healed. (Isaiah 53:4,5)

Not only has he made our sinfulness his own, but he has also entered into something from which we all suffer, the experience of each other's sin. When we reckoned him like a leper, we were putting on him our common and painful experience of being cast out of the group, of being the one who suffers from the sin of others. As Francis found, we each need to welcome that leper as a brother or sister, as a part of ourselves, one of our family. This may not mean welcoming the leper back into the group; it is more likely to mean leaving the group in order to join the leper. This is what Christ did. Yet Francis found, as we do, that once he had allied himself to the outcast, all the world again became his brother and sister. This was not just chance, or even the result of a psychological shift within himself, but rather that he, in sharing his lot with the outcast, was doing what God has done for us all.

In those terrible years after Francis' death, Clare entered deeply into the experience of darkness and sin, both her own and others'. New depths were gouged out in her by the glacier of events, but no growth is painless. The great Sufi mystic, Al-Ghazali, used to say that the entry into each major spiritual stage is preceded by a period of suffering. Certainly Clare's spiritual growth bears this out, and how could she be a teacher for us unless she had the same psychological patterns as the rest of us? She only differs from us in not taking back what she has once offered, nor did she ever forget that even her self-

giving was a gift of grace. We must often seem to God like
drowning people fighting our rescuer. It makes good sense that
growth involves pain, because every transition must begin with
loss of what has gone before, and this we shrink from. Yet having
set out to follow Christ the Way, we have embarked on a road
so steeped in paradox that even we travellers fail to understand
how death can be life, loss be gain or poverty become riches.
Nor can we understand how the infinite relates to our littleness,
yet so it is. Very soon, our own experience will begin to bear
this out, and it is (and is meant to be) an encouragement for us.

Gazing at Christ and considering his life, suspended between
his poverty in the crib and on the cross, we are led, almost in
spite of ourselves, to share in his risen life. Christ is a ring
binding us to God, a ring so moulded that our troubles are set
within it like honoured jewels, wounds in the hands and feet of
God. As we move deeper and deeper into his passion, we come
at last to something so profound that it is beyond our understanding, namely that at his moment of deepest trouble and
most profound abandonment by God, Christ spoke only to God:
'My God, my God, why have you deserted me?' (Matthew 27:47).
This must surely be a moment when the deepest gulfs between
us and God were bridged and healed. After this experience of
Christ's, there is nowhere in the human heart from which we
cannot speak to God. Even that place where God seems to have
deserted us (rather than we God), even that has now become
a place from which we can speak to God. Our deepest hells
have been harrowed and sown. We know now that the grain of
wheat has fallen even into that barren ground. There it died,
and if we wait, the blade will sprout within the ear. When we
climb mountains of despair, we know that even from the pit of
those impenetrable valleys, Christ has spoken to the Source
of life. By passing through those places, he has opened them
to God's luminous light.

> Therefore, contemplate the unimaginable love through which
> Christ was willing to suffer on the Tree of the cross and, on that
> same Tree, to die the most disgraceful kind of death. Then may
> you always catch fire more and more strongly from this burning
> love![14]

The Christ on the San Damiano crucifix pictures much of
this. The mighty figure of the Lord stretches out his arms over

all the groups of people, great and small, all painted on the same block of wood as he is. He is like a great Christ-shaped window to those people and, having once seen him, they can never see life in the way they did before. Light has entered and cannot be denied. Once we have seen this clearly, says Clare, then we can run without stopping until he has brought us into his wine-cellar.[15] There he floods us with kindliness, fills us with sweetness and is like a gentle light glowing in the dark places of our memories.[16] Suffering on the tree of the cross, Christ is God's wisdom spoken in ordinary words of pain, loss and death. The redemptive dimension of the mystery is that by actually becoming those terrible words, Christ introduces into our vocabulary the Word of God, which translates into things like joy, vision, wonder, trust, love, fire and delight. Christ, who never hid his face from the things our words can say, has entered right into the heart of life so that even annihilating suffering can now become pregnant with redemption. When that moment has matured within our hearts, we may hear from within only the clamour of our pain, cried from the tower of our unreality, but everything around us will speak of God. In the same way, Christ does not halt the dreadful things we do to each other, or end the anguish that rends the fabric of our world so that Mother Earth quails and Brother Sun hides his face to cover his emotion. Only, the torturing cord around Juniper's head is the crown of thorns.

12

The Fullness of Light

❖

Through Death, O Lord, be praised,
through our Sister Death,
our Sister Death of the body.*

Death seems to be as taboo today as sex was a hundred years ago and yet, in a cliché, it is one of our few certainties. It never fails to fascinate us, sometimes to the extent of dominating our hearts and cultures. Spiritual and non-spiritual writers alike insist on its significance and yet, like birth (another act of total significance) we have no practice for it except, perhaps, in the pain of our farewells. So we inevitably approach its border country with some degree of apprehension, wondering if we will know what to do. Like the rest of us, Francis thought more about death as his own life drew to a close and, like many extroverts, he did his thinking out loud. He saw that there are, in fact, two deaths: there is the death which leads to life and the death which has nothing else to follow. This last is the terrible logical consequence of living pointlessly. Or, which comes to the same thing in the end, it is the terrible, logical consequence of having made ourselves the point of our lives. Living in this way leaves us with no future, nowhere to go, because we have eroded the distinctions between the journey and the arrival. We have elevated the journey into an end in itself, and robbed the arrival of any point. Such pointlessness so corrodes us from within that it can only lead to the death which has nothing else to follow.

Such pointlessness is possible for us all because of our innate sinfulness. How terrible for those who have died already from sin, said Francis. This sin in us exerts a magnetic tug to which none of us immune. Pointless – or self-centred – living is exactly like endlessly circling the roundabout instead of entering on the road which leads into our future. This roundabout of ourselves rapidly turns into a moral and psychological maze in which we

* Francis: *Canticle of Creation.*

120

become more and more entangled, more and more lost. Yet it is a work of God's mercy that this roundabout always has, leading out of it, a road, a path, a track, however overgrown. It leads from this roundabout of death as termination, with nothing else to follow, to the other death which is a culmination of all that has gone before. This is Death our Sister, as Francis so graciously called her.

When the time for Death our Sister, came for Clare, she had already been ill for many years, so Sister Death may well have seemed like a long-awaited friend, one who had sent many messengers ahead to tell of her coming. In their relation of her death, the contemporary sources almost seem to give us two accounts, as if Clare were operating on two different levels. On one level, she waited anxiously for news from Perugia of Innocent IV's approval of her Rule, and when it finally came, only just in time, she kissed it ardently again and again. She gave it to her sisters, begging them to keep it faithfully. She was then content to go. Her form of life was assured by this approval, her dedication to poverty had finally been articulated in a way the Church was willing to approve.

On the other level, a few days before the end, she withdrew her attention from daily affairs and began to speak quietly with herself. The sisters, not quite catching her words, asked to whom she was speaking. 'I am speaking to my soul' she said, and we realise that, almost for the first time, we are being made privy to that most intimate of dialogues, the way Clare speaks to herself. 'Go calmly and in peace' she tells herself, and just as, at the start of her journey, we had been left to deduce her moments of apprehension, so now here. She spells nothing out, yet it does seem that she is reassuring herself. 'You will have a good escort,' she reminds herself, 'because he who created you has sent you the Holy Spirit. He who created you has made you holy and loved you with a tender love.' The Spirit is the one who made her holy and taught her God's holy manner of working, the one who was still at work, in her and with her. Her words speak to us of such an intimate tenderness with God that we realise, all over again, the intense quality of her prayer and the amazing way she had maintained that intensity all these years. There had been no falling off with time, no lessening of fervour through custom. All her life, she followed her own advice: 'Hold what you now hold, do what you are now doing and do not stop'. She has gone ahead of us, stepping 'with joy and speed, treading cautiously along the narrow path of blessedness'.[1]

Her sister Agnes, back from Florence, was there, drowned in tears. 'Stop crying' said Clare in that elder-sisterly way she had always used towards Agnes, and adds: 'It is pleasing to God that I depart.' Then she echoes Francis' words to herself all those years before, when he had told her that she would see him again and be greatly comforted because of him. She tells Agnes that she, Agnes, will also die soon, and that the Lord will greatly comfort her after Clare has gone; and in fact Agnes died only a few days after Clare, just as she had left home only a few days after Clare. Innocent IV came in person from nearby Perugia just before Clare's death (and before approving her Rule) and gave her absolution, wishing that he had as little need of forgiveness. Brother Raynaldo encouraged her to patience and she replied 'in a very unrestrained voice' that since Francis had taught her about the grace of the Lord Jesus, nothing had been any bother, nothing had been too difficult to bear. The torrent of her love had gladly swept such things before it.

All the strands from the beginning were now surfacing again, after long years of being faithfully but quietly honoured. So we find three of the brothers gathered around her bed, beloved companions of herself and Francis. They were Angelo and Leo, who had almost certainly been among those to welcome her with lights and song all those years before and who had witnessed her hair being shorn by Francis. The third brother was Juniper, that excellent jester of the Lord, the one who had been tortured, the one of whom Francis said that he wished he had a forest of such Junipers. As mentally handicapped people often are, Juniper was fully involved in the present moment. Grief would come later. Clare asked him, and we get the impression that this was her custom when they met, if he had anything new for her from the Lord. Juniper responded with 'burning sparks from the furnace of his heart'[2] and Clare was greatly strengthened for her last effort by those burning sparks, set on fire for the final blaze of longing. Leo knelt down by her bed and hiding his face in the bedclothes, 'kissed the bed of the dying woman' says her biographer piously,[3] but surely he was also hiding his pain, seeking some way to express his grief and devotion, his reverence and his love. Angelo mourned and,

typically, comforted others who were also mourning. Clare
continued to speak to herself and God in one rounded communication, caught up, as dying people are, in the vast process
at work within her. At one point, she said to the sisters: 'Do you
see the King of glory as I do?' but they saw nobody beyond
themselves, and looked into the vista of emptiness which would
be theirs when she had gone.

There had always been something in Clare which was not
exactly a death wish, but rather a longing to be totally consumed
for and by God. When news had come, back in 1221, that five
brothers had been martyred in Morocco, her instant response
had been to set off for Morocco herself. When the Saracens had
rampaged at the door, she had said to the sisters: 'If they come,
place me before them' – knowing that this meant certain rape
and probable death, and that the sisters would certainly do no
such thing. Now the moment had finally come when body and
soul could both leap forward into another mode of life. All her
desires were about to be fulfilled. Meanwhile, news of her dying
reached Assisi and the town emptied as everyone flocked to the
little monastery of San Damiano. She was their saint, and they
wept at the thought of losing her, and marshalled a squadron
of soldiers to make sure that while they might lose her to God,
they would not do so to Perugia.

'O Lord,' she said, 'may you who have created me be blessed,'
and the feeling we get is not that it is all coming to an end, but
that it is all beginning. This moment was simply a moment of
intense excitement, the moment for which she had given herself
the good advice of going forward calmly and peacefully because
everything was about to be made clear. It was the complete
opposite of pointlessness, a complete contrast to the Death with
nothing else to follow. This was her final (but not her last)
lesson to us, so that we too can go into the valley of the shadow
of death calmly and in peace. We too shall have a good escort,
the same one as she had – the Holy Spirit, no less. This Holy
Spirit, she reminded herself, had always guarded her as tenderly
as a mother guards the child who loves her.

Long years ago she had fled at midnight from her home, to
join the Son of God in his degradation. She had been
hammered like a nut to release the good fragrance which was
in her, and now she had perfumed all the house of God. She
had confronted the wild beasts in her heart and become a truly

free woman. She had kept the faith and run the course, she had caught fire from the burning desire of the Crucified and given them all a noble example. She had touched an intensity of human love granted to few of us, had survived the terrible glacier of bereavement and come again into the light. Paradise had already begun to be restored in her, and she had become a sign of the new creation. Now she was stepping out securely, joyfully and swiftly to receive her inheritance. She, who had saved Assisi by the burning purity of her heart, died on the feast of their bishop and protector, the great San Rufino. The first mighty patron of that little town in Umbria which has begotten more mighty patrons than anywhere else on earth, gathered his greatest daughter to himself.

The sisters wrote a letter to tell the brothers and sisters around the world. In it they said:

> We tell you – not without tears – that the mirror of the morning star has vanished. The Lady Clare, our leader, mother and teacher, has been taken by the best man, Death. She has left our sight. Even though physically a violent pain wrenches our hearts, yet we stretch out our right hand to the glory of praise . . . for we understand the dance of joy with which the holy spirits are going to meet her . . .[4]

The mirror of the morning star has vanished. Let Francis have the final word, as he always did for Clare:

> How blest for those who are alive in Your most holy will,
> no further death can harm them.[5]

Notes

❖

Primary sources are referred to in the notes as follows:

Regis J. Armstrong OFM, CAP and Ignatius C. Brady OFM (trs. and eds.), *Francis and Clare: The Complete Works* (Paulist Press, New Jersey and SPCK, London, 1982), cited as *Writings*.

Regis J. Armstrong (trs. and ed.), *Clare of Assisi: Early Documents* (Paulist Press, New Jersey, 1988), cited as *Early Documents*.

Marion A. Habig (ed.), *St Francis of Assisi: Writings and Early Biographies. English Omnibus of the Sources for the Life of St Francis* (Franciscan Herald Press [now the Franciscan Press], Chicago, 1973), cited as *Omnibus*.

See also *Claire d'Assise: Ecrits* (Editions du Cerf, Paris, 1985).

The extracts from Clare's writings and from Francis' *Canticle of Creation* have been translated by Sr Frances Teresa OSC. Other passages are quoted with the permission of the copyright holders as indicated in the notes.

INTRODUCTION
1   Bull of Canonisation, 4 (*Early Documents*, p. 178).

CHAPTER 1 LIFE IN ABUNDANCE
1   Chaucer, *Canterbury Tales*, Prologue.
2   Clare, *Letter 1*, 9–20.
3   Clare, *Letter 1*, 30.
4   cf. Francis' *Rule of 1221*, VI, 4.
5   This lovely phrase comes from the intercessions for the feast of St Clare, in the *New Companion to the Breviary* produced by the Carmelites of Indianapolis, 1988.
6   Clare, *Letter 1*, 25.

7   There has been doubt about whether it was 1211 or 1212, but most scholars seem to have settled for the latter. For our purposes, it does not greatly matter.
8   *Life of Clare*, 24 (*Early Documents*, p. 213).
9   Clare, *Letter 1*, 30.

CHAPTER 2 EXODUS

1   Clare, *Letter 4*, 9–15.
2   Clare, *Letter 2*, 10.
3   Clare, *Letter 2*, 7.
4   Clare, *Letter 2*, 12, 14. *Pedibus inoffensis* has a double meaning of not hurting your feet by stumbling and of doing no harm as your feet pass. It is a neat piece of Latin which more or less defeats the English language.
5   *Testament of Clare*, 2, 19.
6   Clare, *Letter 2*, 22.
7   *Method in Theology*, p. 113ff.
8   *Rule of Clare*, VIII, 16.

CHAPTER 3 THE MINOTAUR WITHIN

1   *Life of Clare*, Prologue (*Early Documents*, p. 189).
2   Clare, *Letter 3*, 20.
3   Clare, *Letter 1*, 14.
4   Clare, *Letter 1*, 15, 16, 17.

CHAPTER 4 A NUT BENEATH THE HAMMER

1   *Life of Clare*, 8 (*Early Documents*, p. 197).
2   cf. Clare, *Letter 1*, 5.
3   cf. *Rule of Clare*, IX, 5.
4   cf. *Life of Clare*, 24 (*Early Documents*, p. 213).
5   *Life of Clare*, 25 (*Early Documents*, p. 215).
6   *Life of Clare*, 26 (*Early Documents*, p. 215).

CHAPTER 5 THE BURNING DESIRES OF GOD

1   cf. many contemporary writings, such as *O clara luce clarior*, a hymn in her honour.
2   Giordano da Giano, *Chronica*, 14; quoted in Arnaldo Fortini, *Francis of Assisi* (Crossroad, New York, 1985), p. 454.
3   Clare, *Letter 1*, 6, 7, 12, 13.
4   *Rule of Clare*, VII, 1.
5   Clare, *Letter 1*, 13. Unless otherwise stated, all the quotations in this chapter are from the first letter.
6   *Legend of the Three Companions*, V, 13 (*Omnibus*, p. 903).
7   *Life of Clare*, 36 (author's translation).

8   *Rule of Clare*, III, 1.
9   *Testament of Clare*, 45.
10   Clare, *Letter 1*, 8.

CHAPTER 6 ECHOES OF PARADISE
1   *Testament of Clare*, 4.
2   See Edith van den Goorbergh OSC and Theo Zweerman OFM, *Clara van Assisi* (Van Gorcum, Assen, 1994), pp. 27ff, where this is fully discussed in connection with Clare.
3   *Testament of Clare*, 38, 39
4   cf. Clare, *Letter 1*, 16.
5   *Admonition* II (*Writings*, p. 27).
6   *Testament of Francis*, 14 (*Writings*, p. 154).
7   Philippians 2:6–8.
8   The full text is to be found in *Sacrum Commercium* (*Omnibus*, pp. 1553ff).
9   Dante, *Divina Commedia, Paradiso* XI, 70–77. This is not the place to do so, but it would be interesting to compare Beatrice in the *Paradiso* with the Lady Poverty, since there are such similarities in the robust way they deal with the man they are instructing.
10   Clare, *Letter 4*, 19–23.
11   Clare, *Letter 1*, 32.
12   Clare, *Letter 1*, 5, 6.
13   *Testament of Clare*, 45, 47.
14   Clare, *Letter 1*, 9.

CHAPTER 7 CLEARER THAN LIGHT
1   *Life of Clare*, 6 (*Early Documents*, p. 194).
2   *Testament of Clare*, 25; *Rule of Clare*, VI, 1.
3   Thomas Celano, *Second Life of Francis* (2 Celano), 185 (*Omnibus*, p. 509.
4   *Rule of Clare*, X, 4, 5.
5   *Early Documents*, p. 105.
6   *Life of Clare*, 19 (cf. *Early Documents*, p. 210).
7   cf. Clare, *Letter 1*, 2; *2*, 2, 31, 34; *3*, 2, 4; *4*, 2.
8   *Rule of Clare*, IV, 7.
9   *Life of Clare*. Clare's prayer is dealt with in sections 19–35 (*Early Documents*, pp. 208, 209ff).
10   Clare, *Letter 1*, 14.
11   Francis' *Rule of 1221*, XVI, 10, 22 (*Writings*, p. 122).
12   *Salutation of the Virtues* (*Writings*, p. 152).
13   Clare, *Letter 3*, 6.
14   Thomas Traherne, *Centuries of Meditations*, I, 60 (Faith Press).

15   *Life of Clare*, 6, (*Early Documents*, p. 194).
16   *Life of Clare*, 18 (*Early Documents*, p. 208).
17   *Testament of Clare*, 18–23.
18   *Rule of Clare*, VI, 2.

CHAPTER 8 A NOBLE EXAMPLE
1   Clare, *Letter 1*, 3, 4.
2   cf. *Life of Clare*, 10 (*Early Documents*, p. 200).
3   ibid.
4   Clare, *Letter 1*, 19, 20.
5   *Testament of Clare*, 21.
6   Clare, *Letter 3*, 8.
7   cf. Clare, *Letter 3*, 11, 12.
8   Bull of Canonisation, 4 (*Early Documents*, p. 178).
9   *Rule of Clare*, VI, 15; *Testament of Clare*, 55.
10   *Life of Clare*, 13 (*Early Documents*, p. 204).
11   Clare, *Letter 1*, 27, 28.
12   ibid., 28.
13   Clare, *Letter 1*, 29.
14   Clare, *Letter 1*, 25–30.
15   *Rule of Clare*, IX, 7–10.
16   Clare, *Letter 4*, 21.
17   Clare, *Letter 4*, 24, 25.
18   Clare, *Letter 1*, 12, 24.
19   *Rule of Clare*, VI, 3.
20   *Rule of St Benedict*, III, 3.
21   *Rule of Clare*, II, 2.
22   *Rule of Clare*, X, 9, 10.

CHAPTER 9 CLARE AND FRANCIS
1   cf. *Testament of Clare*, 37; *Rule of Clare*, I, 2.
2   *Testament of Clare*, 12–14.
3   1 Celano, 18 (*Omnibus*, p. 244).
4   *Legend of the Three Companions*, 69 (*Omnibus*, p. 953).
5   *Life of Clare*, 10 (*Early Documents*, p. 198).
6   *Testament of Clare*, 38.
7   St Bonaventure; cf. *Omnibus*, p. 837.
8   *Life of Clare*, 8 (*Early Documents*, p. 197).
9   *Life of Clare*, 11 (*Early Documents*, p. 201, which should read 'The news of such things' (*tantarum novitas rerum*).
10   cf. *Omnibus*, p. 1333.
11   *Rule of Clare*, VI, 4.
12   cf. Fortini, pp. 364ff.
13   *Mirror of Perfection*, 108 (*Omnibus*, p. 1246).

14   1 Celano, 117 (*Omnibus*, p. 331).
15   *Testament of Clare*, 38, 39.
16   *Testament of Clare*, 38.
17   *Sacrum Commercium*, 25 (*Omnibus*, p. 1566).

CHAPTER 10 THE RESTORATION OF PARADISE

1   *Sacrum Commercium*, 68 (*Omnibus*, p. 1595).
2   cf. Marco Bartoli, *Clare of Assisi*, ch 7; Margaret Carney OSF, *The First Franciscan Woman*, p. 54; Gary Dickson, 'Clare's Dream' in *Mediaevistik*, 5 (1992); Ingrid Peterson OSF, *Clare of Assisi: A Biographical Study*, pp. 186ff.
3   Clare, *Letter 1*, 4: *servitium Iesu Christi*.
4   *Rule of Clare*, VIII, 16.
5   *Salutation of the Blessed Virgin Mary* (*Writings*, p. 149).
6   cf. Antiphon to Our Lady in the Office of the Passion, which Francis compiled and which Clare often prayed (*Writings*, p. 82).
7   *Second Letter to all the Faithful* (*Writings*, p. 67).
8   Clare, *Letter 3*, 18, 19.
9   Clare, *Letter 1*, 8.

CHAPTER 11 CHRIST OUR WAY

1   cf. Clare, *Letter 4*, 18.
2   *Life of Clare*, 44 (*Early Documents*, p. 228; my own translation).
3   This was Niccolò di Giovanni Cocco, leader of Viterbo from 1224 to 1227, when he was torn to pieces by the citizens for betraying his city to the Romans.
4   *Life of Clare* (*Early Documents*, p. 228).
5   2 Celano, 52 (*Omnibus*, p. 409).
6   See also *Life of Clare*, 59 (*Early Documents*, p. 238).
7   cf. Clare, *Letter 4*, 9–14.
8   Clare, *Letter 1*, 32.
9   Clare, *Letter 4*, 18.
10 Clare, *Letter 2*, 20.
11 Clare, *Letter 4*, 23.
12 Clare, *Letter 2*, 11.
13 *Admonition* V (*Writings*, p. 29).
14 Clare, *Letter 4*, 23, 27.
15 Clare, *Letter 4*, 31.
16 Clare, *Letter 4*, 11–13.

CHAPTER 12 THE FULLNESS OF LIGHT

1   Clare, *Letter 2*, 11, 13.
2   *Life of Clare*, 45 (*Early Documents*, p. 228).

3   ibid.
4   Notification of Death (*Early Documents*, p. 122).
5   Francis of Assisi, *The Canticle of Creation* (my translation).

Other Sources

❖

Greyfriars Review, vol. 2, no. 3 (North American Capuchin
Conference).

Arnoldo Fortini, *Francis of Assisi* (Crossroad, New York, 1985).

Marco Bartoli (trs. Sr Frances Teresa osc), *Clare of Assisi*
(Darton, Longman & Todd, London, 1993).

Raoul Manselli, *San Francesco* (Bulzoni, 1982); trs. Paul Duggan,
(Franciscan Herald Press, 1988).

Raphael Brown (trs.), *The Little Flowers of St Francis* (Doubleday,
New York, 1958).